SURVIVAL ENGLISH

ENGLISH THROUGH CONVERSATIONS

BOOK 1

Lee Mosteller

Bobbi Paul
Kearny Adult Center

Illustrated by Jesse Gonzales

 Prentice Hall Regents, Englewood Cliffs, NJ 07632

Library of Congress Cataloging in Publication Data

MOSTELLER, LEE.
  Survival English.

    1. English language—Textbooks for foreign speakers.
2. English language—Conversation and phrase books.
I. Paul, Bobbi. II. Title.
PE1128.M743 1985   428.3'4   83-26952
ISBN 0-13-879172-4

Editorial/production supervision and
  interior design: Patricia V. Amoroso
Cover design: Lundgren Graphics, Ltd.
Manufacturing buyer: Harry P. Baisley
Page layout: Toni Sterling

Printed in the United States of America

10 9

ISBN 0-13-879172-4   01

PRENTICE-HALL INTERNATIONAL, INC., *London*
PRENTICE-HALL OF AUSTRALIA PTY. LIMITED, *Sydney*
EDITORA PRENTICE-HALL DO BRASIL, LTDA., *Rio de Janeiro*
PRENTICE-HALL CANADA INC., *Toronto*
PRENTICE-HALL OF INDIA PRIVATE LIMITED, *New Delhi*
PRENTICE-HALL OF JAPAN, INC., *Tokyo*
PRENTICE-HALL OF SOUTHEAST ASIA PTE. LTD., *Singapore*
WHITEHALL BOOKS LIMITED, *Wellington, New Zealand*

CONTENTS

*Note on Unit 2: The dialogues, exercises, and vocabulary in the General ID unit are designed as supplementary materials for the other units. For example, page 55 in General ID may be used in conjunction with Health 7, page 99. Money (pages 61–64) can be taught and reviewed in the units on transportation, food, clothing, housing, occupations, and community. These concepts take more than one lesson to develop and need constant reinforcement. We suggest you spend some time each class on this unit, while continuing with the other units. You may begin this unit concurrently with Personal ID.

10 COMMUNITY 222

PREFACE

This workbook has been designed by teachers of beginning ESL students. It is aimed towards students who have some degree of literacy and does not address preliterate skills. To be successful with this book, students should have a small oral vocabulary and a knowledge of our alphabet.

The main objective of *Survival English* is to teach the most basic functional English patterns to these students. The teaching consists of many small steps that are simple, direct, and repetitive. Because of this, a few of the dialogues will not be conversationally functional. However, the book will provide a vocabulary and structure background in which new knowledge can be integrated.

Theoretically we agree that beginning students should have generous time to develop listening skills before being expected to produce language. However, the need exists to teach literacy as soon as possible along with oral skills, and as adults, these students want to read and write immediately.

Included in each unit is a variety of exercises to reinforce the oral patterns and to teach listening, speaking, reading, and writing. Reading and writing are introduced after the student has mastered oral patterns. This book is based on the theory that students learn to speak English by listening, speaking, reading, and writing, in that order.

OBJECTIVES

1. To teach the most basic functional language patterns in survival situations
2. To teach language patterns and vocabulary in a systematic and controlled manner
3. To develop reading and writing skills based on what the student can produce orally
4. To provide survival information and coping skills necessary for adult living.

ACKNOWLEDGMENTS

Our special thanks to Gretchen Bitterlin, ESL Chairperson, San Diego Community Colleges, for her encouragement and suggestions.

1

PERSONAL ID

ESSENTIAL VOCABULARY _____

1. good morning
   how are you
   I'm fine
   thank you
   thanks
   afternoon
   evening

2. is
   she
   busy
   she's
   they
   they're
   happy
   tired
   hot
   cold
   sad
   angry

3. am
   he

4. isn't
   aren't
   no

5. not

6. what's
   her
   name
   Ann Lee
   his
   Bob Jones
   first
   last

7. your
   my
   spell that
   please

8. address
   Main Street
   telephone number
   social security number

9. (review)

10. city
    state
    country
    zip code
    what

11. from
Mexico
Carbo

12. old
birth date
it's
year
month
January
February
March
April
May

June
July
August
September
October
November
December

13. married
widowed
husband
died

14. single
divorced

PERSONAL 1

Name _____

A. Good morning.
    How are you?

B. I'm fine, thank you.
    How are you?

A. Fine, thanks.

Good morning.

Good afternoon.

Good evening.

I

we

he

you

she

they

PERSONAL 2

Name _____

A. How is she?
B. She's busy.
A. How are they?
B. They're fine.

Match

1. fine

2. busy

3. tired

4. hot

5. cold

6. happy

7. sad

8. angry

5

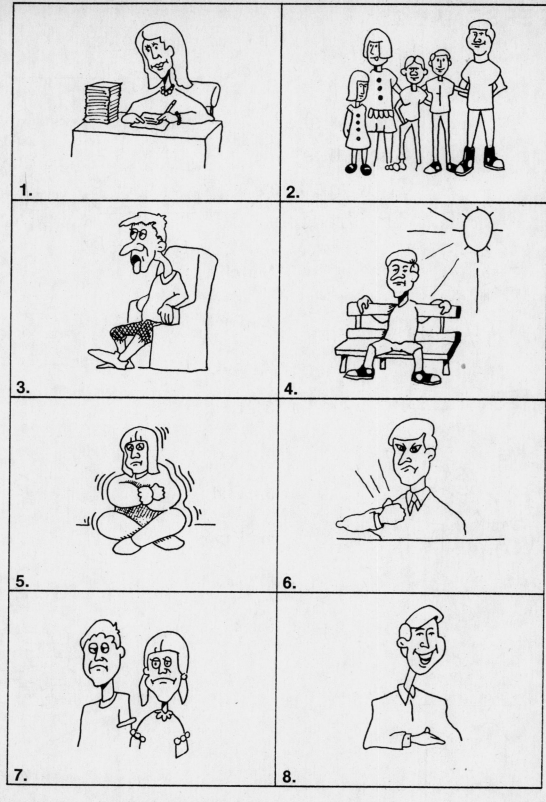

He's   She's   They're   I'm   fine   busy
tired   hot   cold   happy   sad   angry

1. How is she?

   _____ cold.

2. How is he?

   _____ tired.

3. How are they?

   _____ fine.

4. How is he?

   _____ hot.

5. How is she?

    She's _____.

6. How are they?

    They're _____.

7. How is he?

    He's _____.

8. How is he?

    He's _____.

How	are	you they	?
	is	he she	

I'm They're	fine.
He's She's	

1. How is he? _____ _____.

2. How are they? _____ _____.

3. How are you? _____ _____.

4. How is she? _____ _____.

5. How are they? _____ _____.

6. How is he? _____ _____.

7. How are you? _____ _____.

8. How is she? _____ _____.

PERSONAL 3

Name _____

A. Are you busy?
B. Yes, I am.
A. Is he tired?
B. Yes, he is.

Yes,	I	am
	he she	is
	they	are

1. Is she busy?

    Yes, _____ _____.

2. Is he tired?

Yes, _____ _____.

3. Are they sad?

Yes, _____ _____.

4. Are you busy?

Yes, _____ _____.

PERSONAL 4

Name _____

A. Is he sad?
B. No, he isn't.
A. Are they happy?
B. No, they aren't.

No,	he she	isn't
	they	aren't

1. Is he happy?

No, _____ _____ .

2. Are they sad?

No, _____ _____ .

3. Is she hot?

No, _____ _____.

4. Is he angry?

No, _____ _____.

Yes,	she he	is
	they	are

1. Is he happy?

Yes, _____ he _____ _____ is _____.

2. Is he tired?

Yes, _____ _____.

3. Are they sad?

   Yes, _____ _____.

4. Is she busy?

   Yes, _____ _____.

| No, | he
she | isn't |
| | they | aren't |

5. Is he cold?

   No, _____ he _____ _____ isn't _____.

6. Are they angry?

    No, _____ _____.

7. Is he hot?

    No, _____ _____.

8. Is she fine?

    No, _____ _____.

PERSONAL 5

Name _____

A.   Are you busy?
B.   No, I'm not.

1.   Are you busy? No, I'm not.
2.   Are you angry? No, I'm _____.
3.   Are you cold? No, I'm _____.
4.   Are you hot? No, _____ _____.
5.   Are you sad? _____, _____ _____.
6.   Are you fine? Yes, I am.
7.   Are you busy? Yes, I _____.
8.   Are you happy? Yes, I _____.
9.   Are you tired? Yes, _____ _____.
10. Are you cold? _____, _____ _____.

PERSONAL 6

Name _____

A. What's her name?
B. Her first name is Ann.
   Her last name is Lee.

A. What's his name?
B. His first name is Bob.
   His last name is Jones.

| His |
| Her |

1. _____ name is Bob Jones.

2. _____ name is Ann Lee.

3. His _____ name is Bob.

4. His _____ name is Jones.

5. Her _____ name is Ann.

6. Her _____ name is Lee.

PERSONAL 7

First name _____

A. What's your name?
B. My name is _____.
A. What's your first name?
B. My first name is _____.
A. Spell that.
B. _____
A. What's your last name?
B. My last name is _____.
A. Please spell that.
B. _____

First name _____
Last name _____

LAST NAME _____
FIRST NAME _____

Name _____
          Last   First

a a _____

b b _____

c c _____

d d _____

e e _____

f f _____

g g _____

h h _____

i i _____

j j _____

k k _____

l l _____

m m _____

n n _____

o o _____

p p _____

q q _____

r r _____

s s _____

t t _____

u u _____

v v _____

w w _____

x x _____

y y _____

z z _____

A A _____

B B _____

C C _____

D D _____

E E _____

F F _____

G G _____

H H _____

I I _____

J J _____

K K _____

L L _____

M M _____

N N _____

O O _____

P P _____

Q Q _____

R R _____

S S _____

T T _____

U U _____

V V _____

W W _____

X X _____

Y Y _____

Z Z _____

PERSONAL 8

Last name _____

A. What's his address?

B. 7613 Main Street.

A. What's his telephone number?

B. 560-6660

A. What's his social security number?

B. 560-58-8025

Match

1. address
2. telephone number
3. social security number
4. address
5. telephone number
6. address
7. social security number
8. telephone number
9. address
10. social security number
11. telephone number
12. address

PERSONAL 9

First name _____

name _____

_____

A. **What's your address?**

B. _____

A. **What's your telephone number?**

B. _____

A. **What's your social security number?**

B. _____

Name _____   NAME _____

Add. _____   ADDRESS _____

Tel. _____   TELEPHONE _____

Soc. Sec. No. _____ - ___ - _____   SOCIAL SECURITY _____ - ___ - _____

name _____   Name _____

address _____   Address _____

telephone _____   Telephone _____

social security _____ - ___ - _____   Social Security _____ - ___ - _____

PERSONAL 10

First name _____

Bob Jones
7613 Main Street
San Diego CA 92111
U.S.A.

A. **What's your address?**

B. _____

A. **What city?**

B. _____

A. **What state?**

B. _____

A. **What country?**

B. _____

A. **What's your zip code?**

B. _____

address _____

city _____

state _____

zip code _____

```
┌─────────────────────────────────────────────────────┐
│  Name _____ │
│              first              last                 │
│  Address _____ │
│          _____   │
│            city           state          zip code   │
│  Telephone number _____  │
│                                                      │
│  Social security number _____ - ____ - _____  │
└─────────────────────────────────────────────────────┘
```

1. My first name is _____.

2. My last name is _____.

3. My address is _____.

4. My telephone number is _____.

5. My zip code is _____.

6. My social security number is _____ - ____ - _____.

7. My city is _____.

8. My state is _____.

9. My country is _____.

Match

first name	560-58-8025
telephone number	San Diego
zip code	Jones
social security number	7613 Main Street
last name	92111
state	California
country	560-6660
city	U.S.A.
address	Bob

First name _____ Last name _____

Address _____

Country _____ City _____ State _____

Telephone number _____ Zip code _____

Social Security Number _____

last   name   first   name

address   city   state

country   zip code

telephone number

PERSONAL 11

Address _____

A. What country is he from?
B. He's from Mexico.
A. What city is he from?
B. He's from Carbo.
A. What country are you from?
B. I'm from _____.
A. What city are you from?
B. I'm from _____.

I'm from _____, _____.

Name _____

Address _____
      street   city

    _____
      state   zip code

Telephone _____

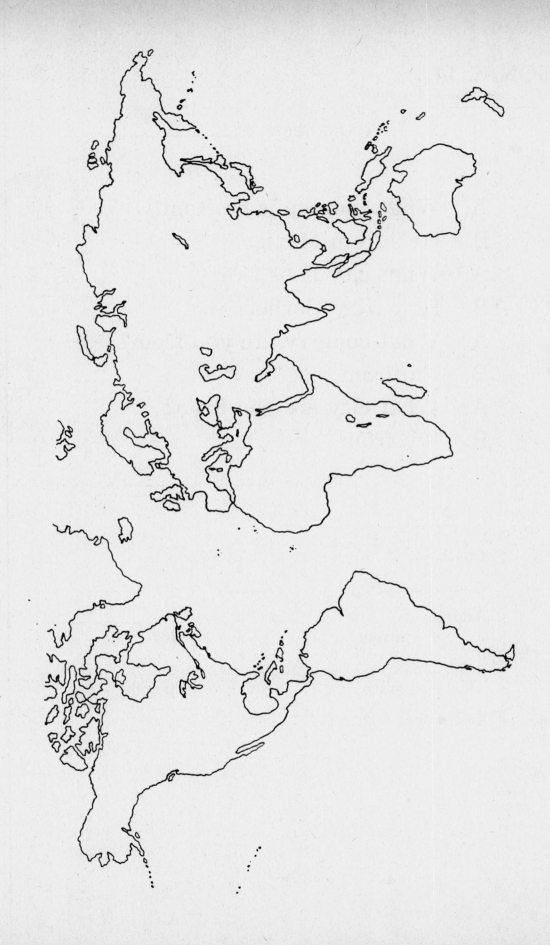

	name	address	zip code	telephone number
	Bob Jones	7613 Main Street	92111	560-6660
	Ann Lee	6514 First Street	74920	896-7531

Zip code _____

A. How old is Bob?

B. He's 35.

A. What's his birth date?

B. It's May 17, 1948.

A. How old are you?

B. I'm _____.

A. What's your birth date?

B. It's _____ _____, 19____.

| | | birth date | | |
name	age	month	day	year
Bob Jones	35	May	17	1948

January
February
March
April
May
June
July
August
September
October
November
December

PERSONAL 13

State _____

A. Is he married?
B. Yes, he is.
A. Is she married?
B. No, she isn't.
She's widowed.
Her husband died.

Yes	he she	is
	they	are

No	he she	isn't
	they	aren't

1. Is he married?

Yes _____ _____.

2. Is he widowed?

No _____ _____.

3. Are they married?

Yes _____ _____.

4. Is she widowed?

Yes _____ _____.

5. Is she married?

No _____ _____.

PERSONAL 14

Telephone number _____

A. Is she married?
B. No, she isn't.
   She's single.
A. Is he married?
B. No, he isn't.
   He's divorced.
A. Are you married?
B. _____.

1. Is she married?
   No, _____ _____.
2. Is she single?
   Yes, _____ _____.

3. Is he divorced?
   No, _____ _____.
4. Is he married?
   Yes, _____ _____.

5. Are they married?
   No, _____ _____.
6. Are they divorced?
   Yes, _____ _____.

7. Are you married?

_____, _____ _____.

Sue and Joe are married.
They're happy.
They're from Mexico.

1. Is Sue married?

   _____.

2. Is Joe married?

   _____.

3. Is Joe happy?

   _____.

4. Is Joe single?

   _____.

5. Is Sue single?

   _____.

6. What country are they from?

   _____.

7. Are they from Mexico?

   _____.

	single	widowed	divorced	married
Ann		✔		
Kim			✔	
Lee	✔			
Bob				✔

1. Is Bob married?

2. Is Bob divorced?

3. Is Lee single?

4. Is Lee married?

5. Is Ann divorced?

6. Is Ann widowed?

7. Is Kim married?

8. Is Kim single?

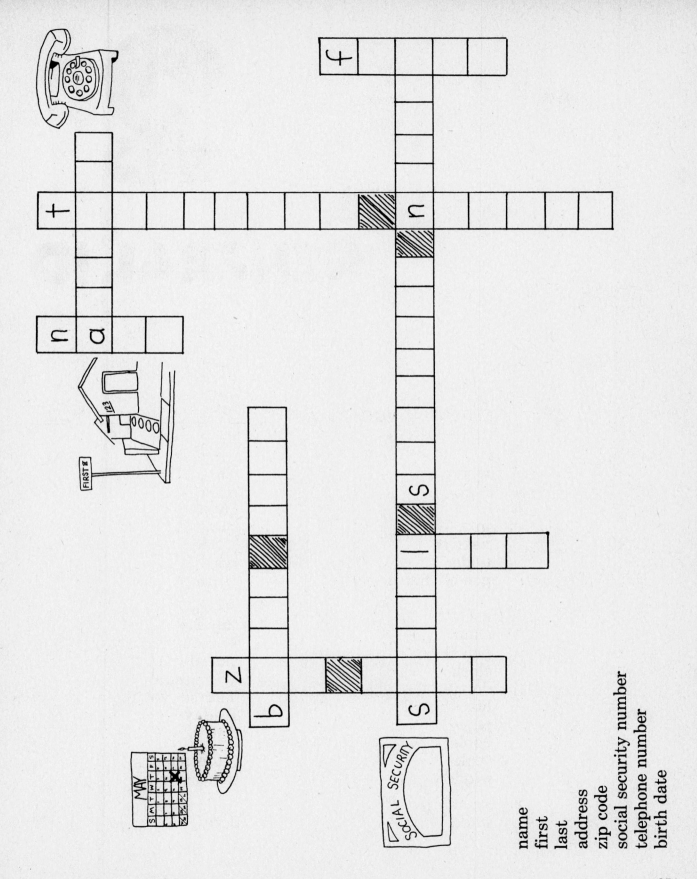

name
first
last
address
zip code
social security number
telephone number
birth date

2

GENERAL ID

ESSENTIAL VOCABULARY _____

1. where's
   the
   on
   in
   next to
   under
   pencil sharpener
   pen
   light
   chair
   pencil
   clock
   door
   blackboard
   paper
   book
   table
   window

2. stand up
   walk

   close
   open
   go out
   come in
   sit down
   read
   write

3. today
   Sunday
   Monday
   Tuesday
   Wednesday
   Thursday
   Friday
   Saturday

4. yesterday
   tomorrow
   was

5. date

6. weather
   how's
   sunny
   rainy
   cloudy
   hot
   cold

7. excuse me
   time
   class
   at

8. need
   penny
   nickel
   dime
   quarter
   dollar

1.	2.	3.
4.	5.	6.
7.	8.	9.
10.	11.	12.

pencil sharpener   pencil   paper
pen   clock   book
light   door   table
chair   blackboard   window

GENERAL 1

Name _____

A. Where's the _____?

B. It's
| on |
| in |
| next to |
| under |
the _____.

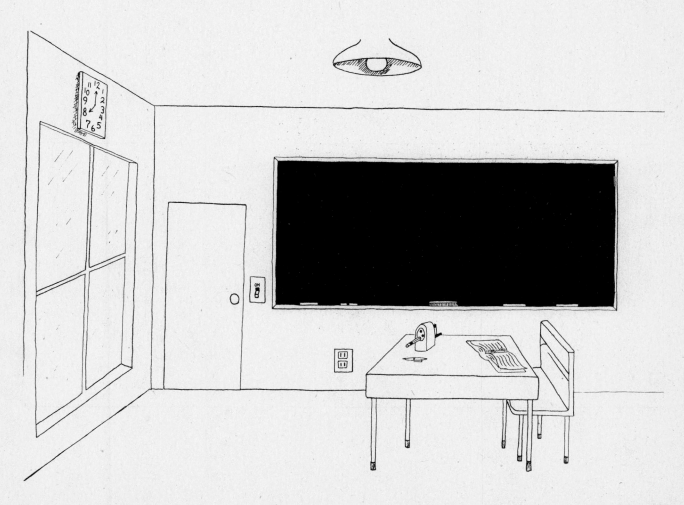

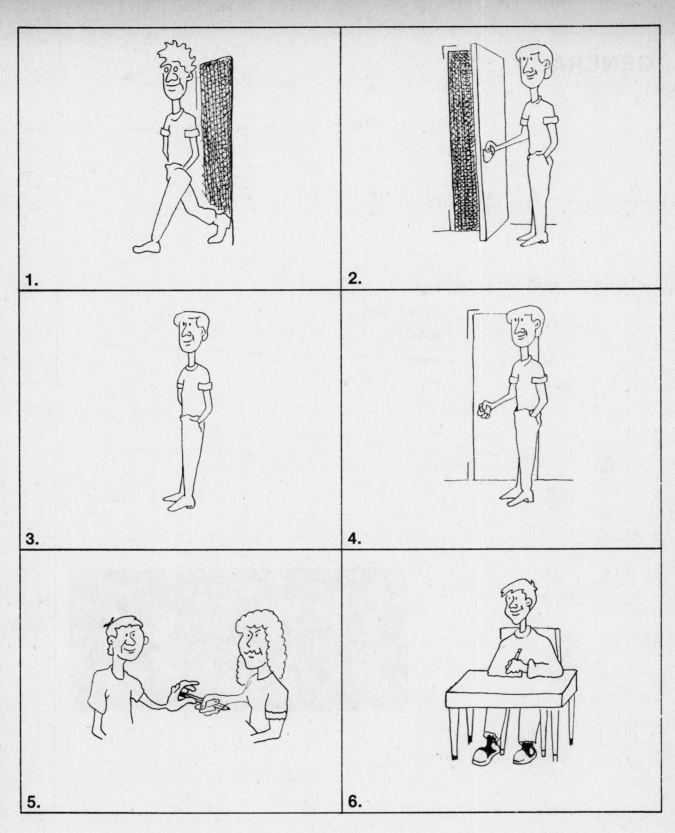

1.

2.

3.

4.

5.

6.

go
open
give

stand
close
write

GENERAL 2

First name _____

1. Please stand up.
2. Please walk to the door.
3. Please open the door.
4. Please go out.
5. Please come in.
6. Please close the door.
7. Please walk to the window.
8. Please open the window.
9. Please close the window.
10. Please walk to your chair.
11. Please sit down.
12. Please open your book.
13. Please read your book.
14. Please close your book.
15. Please write your name.
    Thank you.

_____   _____

_____   _____

_____   _____   _____

1. _____

2. _____

3. _____

4. _____

5. _____

6. _____

7. _____

8. _____

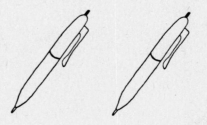

9. _____

10. _____

1. _____ out.

2. _____ up.

3. _____ the door.

4. _____ your name.

5. _____ the door.

6. _____ him a pencil.

43

book
pencil sharpener
blackboard
paper
clock
table
door
light
pen
chair

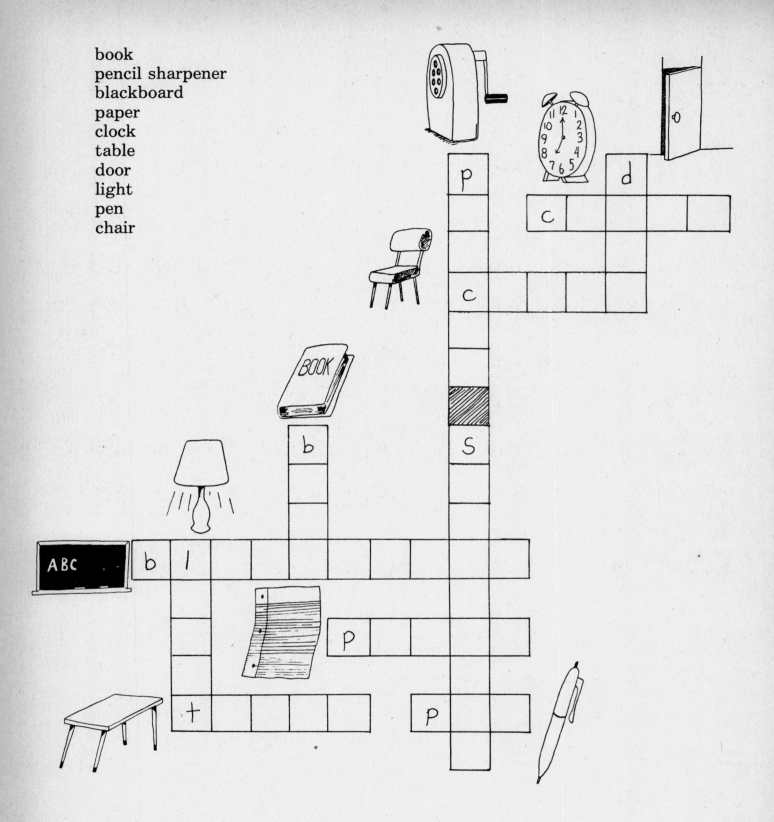

1	2	3	4	5	6	7	8	9	10
11	12	13	14	15	16	17	18	19	20
21	22	23	24	25	26	27	28	29	30
31	32	33	34	35	36	37	38	39	40
41	42	43	44	45	46	47	48	49	50
51	52	53	54	55	56	57	58	59	60
61	62	63	64	65	66	67	68	69	70
71	72	73	74	75	76	77	78	79	80
81	82	83	84	85	86	87	88	89	90
91	92	93	94	95	96	97	98	99	100

See the Teacher's Guide.

0 0
1 1
2 2
3 3
4 4
5 5
6 6
7 7
8 8
9 9
10 10
11 11
12 12
13 13
14 14
15 15
16 16
17 17
18 18
19 19
20 20
30 30
40 40
50 50
60 60
70 70
80 80
90 90
100 100

GENERAL 3

Last name _____

A. What's today?
B. It's _____.

1. Sunday _____ Sun. _____

2. Monday _____ Mon. _____

3. Tuesday _____ Tues. _____

4. Wednesday _____ Wed. _____

5. Thursday _____ Thur. _____

6. Friday _____ Fri. _____

7. Saturday _____ Sat. _____

GENERAL 4

A. What's today?

B. It's _____.

A. What was yesterday?

B. It was _____.

A. What's tomorrow?

B. It's _____.

1. Today is Monday.

   Tomorrow is _____.

2. Today is Wednesday.

   Tomorrow is _____.

3. Today is Friday.

   Tomorrow is _____.

4. Today is Friday.

   Yesterday was _____.

5. Today is Sunday.

   Yesterday was _____.

GENERAL 5

Address _____

A. What's the date?
B. It's _____ _____ _____.

1. January _____ Jan. _____
2. February _____ Feb. _____
3. March _____ Mar. _____
4. April _____ Apr. _____
5. May _____ May _____
6. June _____ Jun. _____
7. July _____ Jul. _____
8. August _____ Aug. _____
9. September _____ Sept. _____
10. October _____ Oct. _____
11. November _____ Nov. _____
12. December _____ Dec. _____

SEPTEMBER

Sun.	Mon.	Tues.	Wed.	Thurs.	Fri.	Sat.
		1	2	3	4	5
6	7	8	9	10	11	12
13	14	15	16	17	18	19
20	21	22	23	24	25	26
27	28	29	30			

See the Teacher's Guide.

1983

JANUARY

						1
2	3	4	5	6	7	8
9	10	11	12	13	14	15
16	17	18	19	20	21	22
23	24	25	26	27	28	29
30	31					

FEBRUARY

	1	2	3	4	5	
6	7	8	9	10	11	12
13	14	15	16	17	18	19
20	21	22	23	24	25	26
27	28					

MARCH

	1	2	3	4	5	
6	7	8	9	10	11	12
13	14	15	16	17	18	19
20	21	22	23	24	25	26
27	28	29	30	31		

APRIL

					1	2
3	4	5	6	7	8	9
10	11	12	13	14	15	16
17	18	19	20	21	22	23
24	25	26	27	28	29	30

MAY

1	2	3	4	5	6	7
8	9	10	11	12	13	14
15	16	17	18	19	20	21
22	23	24	25	26	27	28
29	30	31				

JUNE

			1	2	3	4
5	6	7	8	9	10	11
12	13	14	15	16	17	18
19	20	21	22	23	24	25
26	27	28	29	30		

JULY

					1	2
3	4	5	6	7	8	9
10	11	12	13	14	15	16
17	18	19	20	21	22	23
24	25	26	27	28	29	30
31						

AUGUST

	1	2	3	4	5	6
7	8	9	10	11	12	13
14	15	16	17	18	19	20
21	22	23	24	25	26	27
28	29	30	31			

SEPTEMBER

				1	2	3
4	5	6	7	8	9	10
11	12	13	14	15	16	17
18	19	20	21	22	23	24
25	26	27	28	29	30	

OCTOBER

						1
2	3	4	5	6	7	8
9	10	11	12	13	14	15
16	17	18	19	20	21	22
23	24	25	26	27	28	29
30	31					

NOVEMBER

	1	2	3	4	5	
6	7	8	9	10	11	12
13	14	15	16	17	18	19
20	21	22	23	24	25	26
27	28	29	30			

DECEMBER

				1	2	3
4	5	6	7	8	9	10
11	12	13	14	15	16	17
18	19	20	21	22	23	24
25	26	27	28	29	30	31

See the Teacher's Guide.

GENERAL 6

First name _____

A. How's the weather?
B. It's rainy.

sunny
cloudy

rainy
hot/cold

1. How's the weather?

   It's _____.

2. How's the weather?

   It's _____.

3. How's the weather?

   It's _____.

4. How's the weather?

   It's _____.

5. How's the weather?

   It's _____.

6. How's the weather?

   It's _____.

GENERAL 7

Last name _____

A. Excuse me. What time is it?
B. It's 8:00.
A. What time is the class?
B. It's at 8:30.

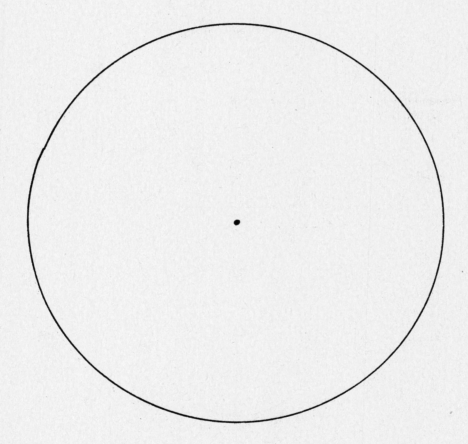

See the Teacher's Guide.

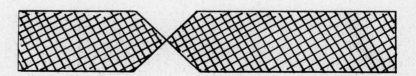

WHAT TIME IS IT?

 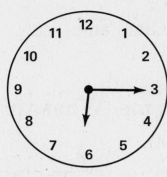 

1. _____ 2. _____ 3. _____

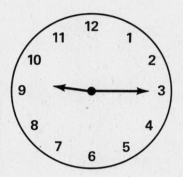 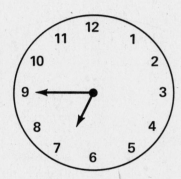 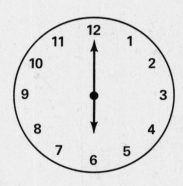

4. _____ 5. _____ 6. _____

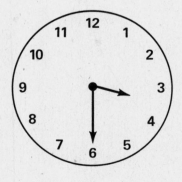  

7. _____ 8. _____ 9. _____

Match

6:15	3:00	9:15
9:45	6:00	6:45
3:45	3:30	9:30

WHAT TIME IS IT?

1. _____

2. _____

3. _____

4. _____

5. _____

6. _____

7. ___ 4:10 ___

8. ___ 7:05 ___

9. ___ 2:40 ___

10. ___ 3:25 ___

11. ___ 12:45 ___

12. ___ 6:50 ___

WHAT TIME IS IT?

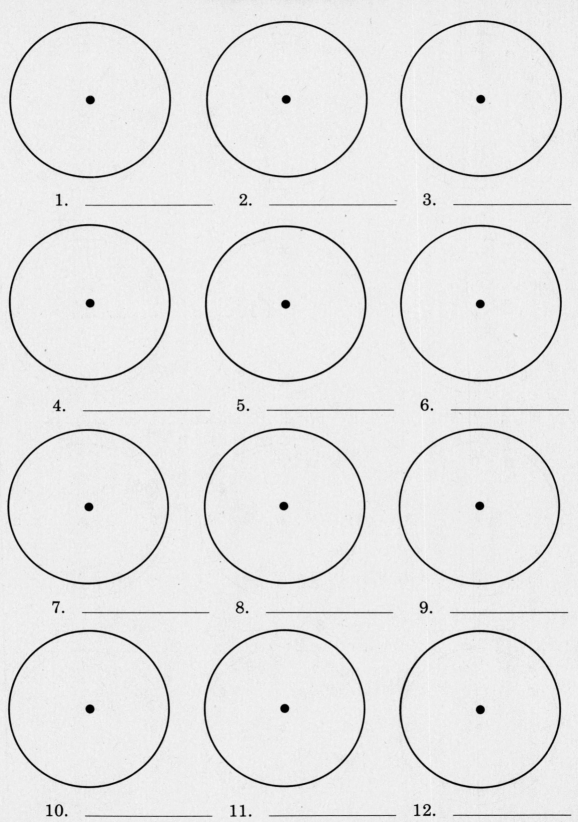

1. _____ 2. _____ 3. _____

4. _____ 5. _____ 6. _____

7. _____ 8. _____ 9. _____

10. _____ 11. _____ 12. _____

		Free		

See the Teacher's Guide.

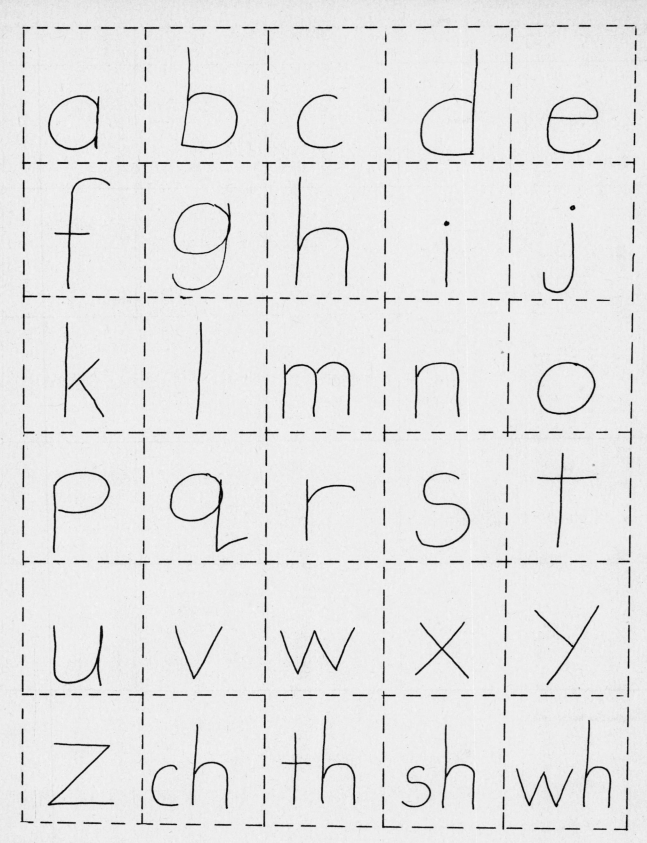

a b c d e

f g h i j

k l m n o

p q r s t

u v w x y

z ch th sh wh

See the Teacher's Guide.

GENERAL 8

Social security number _____

A. I need a _____.

1. quarter
25¢

2. dime
10¢

3. nickel
5¢

4. penny
1¢

5. dollar
$1.00

Match

quarter		$1.00
dime		5¢
penny		10¢
nickel		25¢
dime		1¢
nickel		25¢
quarter		5¢
penny		10¢
dollar		1¢

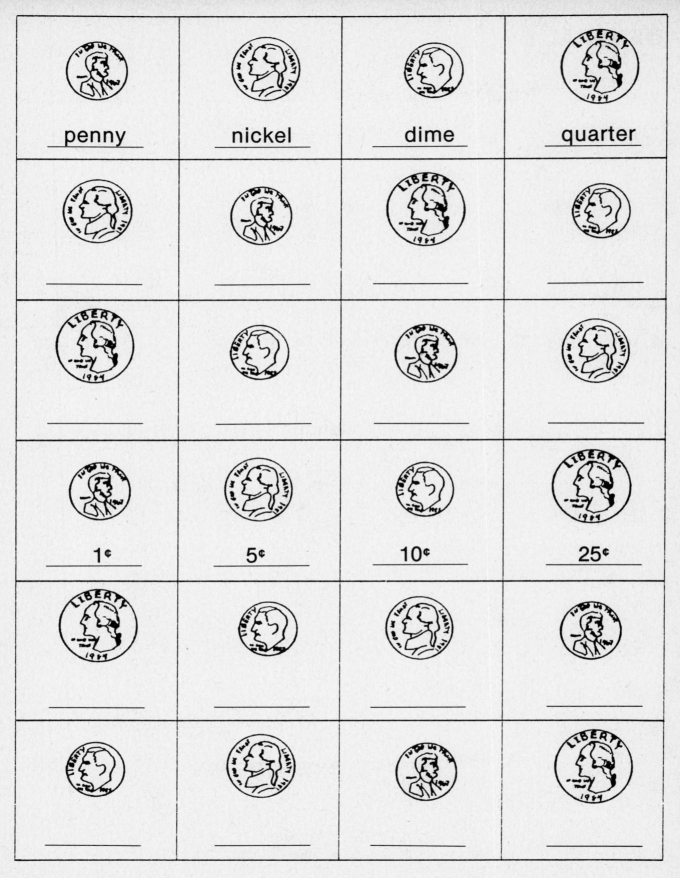

penny	nickel	dime	quarter
1¢	5¢	10¢	25¢

1. __5¢__ __10¢__ __1¢__ __1¢__ = __17¢__

2. _____ _____ _____ _____ = _____

3. _____ _____ _____ _____ = _____

4. _____ _____ _____ _____ = _____

5. _____ _____ _____ _____ = _____

6. _____ _____ _____ _____ = _____

63

Circle correct amount:

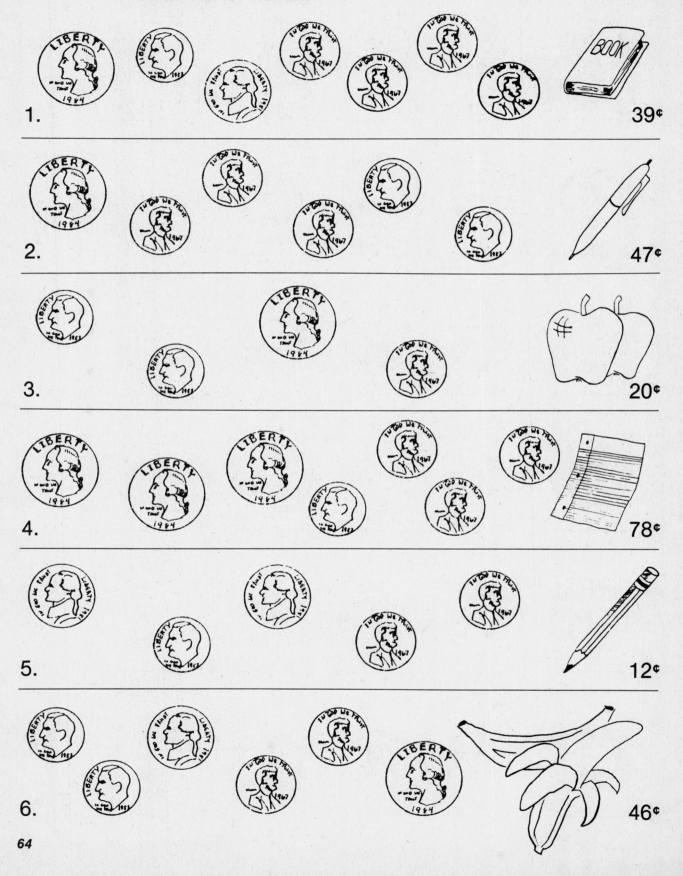

1.   39¢

2.   47¢

3.   20¢

4.   78¢

5.   12¢

6.   46¢

3

FAMILY

ESSENTIAL VOCABULARY _____

1. who's
   wife
   sister
   mother
   father
   brother
   friend
   too

2. husband
   home
   doing
   taking care of
   children
   cooking
   cleaning
   studying

3. doesn't
   does
   have
   how many
   has
   sons
   daughters

4. do
   don't

5. school
   child
   one

6. kindergarten
   elementary
   grade
   teacher
   high school
   junior high
   Mrs.

7. student
   Miss
   Mr.
   Ms.

8. excited
   why
   because
   coming
   parents
   grandparents
   grandsons
   granddaughters
   grandchildren

FAMILY 1

Address _____

A. Who's she?
B. She's my wife.
A. Is she your sister?
B. No, she isn't. She's my mother.
A. Is he your father?
B. No, he isn't. He's my brother.
A. Is he your brother, too?
B. No, he isn't. He's my friend.

mother

brother

friend

wife

husband

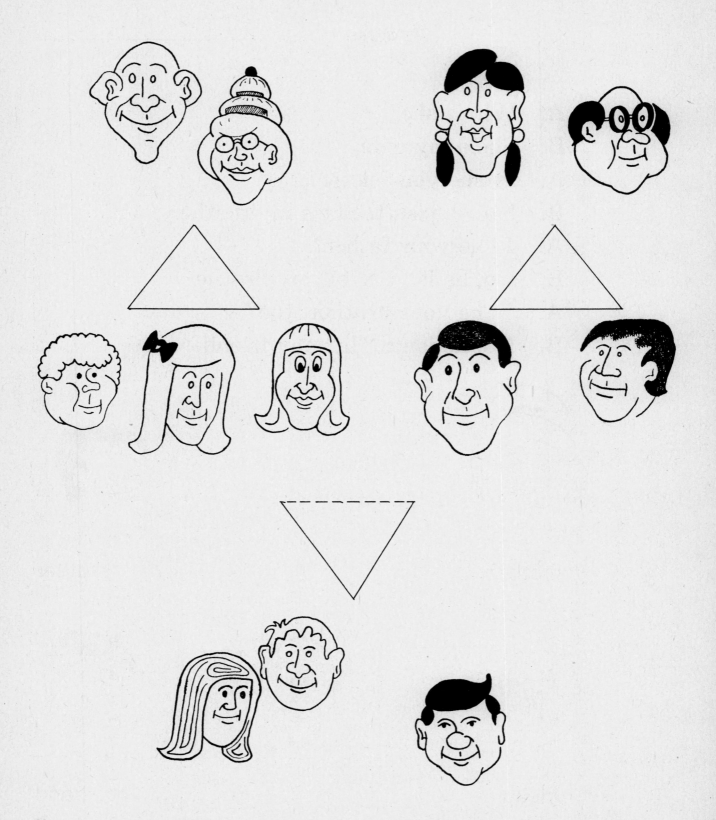

FAMILY 2

A. Where's your husband?
B. He's at home.
A. What's he doing?
B. He's taking care of the children.

taking care of
cooking

cleaning
studying

	Yes,	he she	is.		He's She's

1. Is he at home?

_____, _____ _____.

What's he doing?

_____ _____ _____ _____

_____ _____.

2. Is she at home?

_____, _____ _____.

What's she doing?

_____ _____.

3. Is she at home?

_____, _____ _____.

What's she doing?

_____ _____ _____.

4. Is he at home?

_____, _____ _____.

What's he doing?

_____ _____.

No,	he she	isn't.

1. Is he studying?

   No, _____ _____.

   He's _____ _____ _____

   _____ _____.

2. Is she cleaning the house?

   No, _____ _____.

   She's _____.

3. Is he taking care of the children?

   No, _____ _____.

   He's _____.

4. Is she cooking?

   No, _____ _____.

   She's _____.

FAMILY 3

A. Does he have children?

B. No, he doesn't.

A. Does she have children?

B. Yes, she does.

A. How many children does she have?

B. She has 5 children.
   She has 3 sons and 2 daughters.

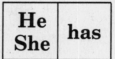

Yes,	he she	does.

He She	has

1. Does she have children?

   _____ , _____ _____ .

2. How many children does she have?

   _____ _____ _____ .

3. Does he have children?

   _____ , _____ _____ .

4. How many children does he have?

   _____ _____ _____ .

FAMILY 4

A. Do you have children?

B. No, I don't. I'm single.
Do you have children?

A. Yes, I do.

B. How many children do you have?

A. I have _____ children.

1. Do you have children?

   _____, I _____.

2. How many children do you have?

   I have _____ _____.

3. Do you have sons?

   _____, I _____.

4. How many sons do you have?

   I have _____ _____.

5. Do you have daughters?

   _____, I _____.

6. How many daughters do you have?

   I have _____ _____.

FAMILY 5

City _____

A. Do you have children?

B. Yes, I do.

A. How old are they?

B. One son is 13.
One daughter is 11.
One daughter is 8.
One son is 2.

A. Are they in school?

B. Yes, 3 children are in school.
One child is at home.

Name	How Many				
	children	sons	daughters	brothers	sisters

1. How many children do they have?

   _____ _____ _____

   _____.

2. How many sons do they have?

   _____ _____ _____

   _____.

3. How many daughters do they have?

   _____ _____ _____

   _____.

4. How many children does he have?

   _____ _____ _____

   _____.

5. How many sons does he have?

   _____ _____ _____

   _____.

6. How many daughters does he have?

   _____ _____ _____

   _____.

7. How many children does she have?

_____ _____ _____

_____.

8. How many sons does she have?

_____ _____ _____

_____.

9. How many daughters does she have?

_____ _____ _____

_____.

10. How many children do you have?

_____ _____ _____

_____.

11. How many sons do you have?

_____ _____ _____

_____.

12. How many daughters do you have?

_____ _____ _____

_____.

FAMILY 6

Telephone _____

A. Is her son in school?

B. Yes, he is.

A. What school?

B. Bayside Elementary School.

A. What grade?

B. 2nd grade.

A. Who's his teacher?

B. Mrs. Walker.

ELEMENTARY SCHOOL	JUNIOR HIGH SCHOOL	HIGH SCHOOL
kindergarten	7th grade	10th grade
1st grade	8th grade	11th grade
2nd grade	9th grade	12th grade
3rd grade		
4th grade		
5th grade		
6th grade		

FAMILY 7

Social security number _____

A. Are you in school?

B. Yes, I am.

A. What school?

B. _____ .

A. Who's your teacher?

B. | Miss | _____ .
    | Mr. |
    | Mrs. |
    | Ms. |

A. Are you a good student?

B. Yes, I am.

1. Are you in school?

    _____ , _____ _____ .

2. What school? _____ .

3. Who's your teacher? _____ .

FAMILY 8

Birth date _____

A. Oh, I'm excited.
B. Why?

A. Because my family is coming.
B. Are your brothers and sisters coming?

A. Yes, they are.
B. How many brothers and sisters do you have?

A. I have 2 brothers and 3 sisters.
B. Are your parents and grandparents coming, too?

A. Yes, they are.
B. I'm excited, too.

1. How many brothers do you have?

    _____ _____ _____ _____.

2. How many sisters do you have?

    _____ _____ _____ _____.

3. How many children do you have?

    _____ _____ _____ _____.

4. How many daughters do you have?

    _____ _____ _____ _____.

5. How many sons do you have?

    _____ _____ _____ _____.

6. How many grandchildren do you have?

    _____ _____ _____ _____.

7. How many granddaughters do you have?

    _____ _____ _____ _____.

8. How many grandsons do you have?

    _____ _____ _____ _____.

1. My name is _____.

2. I'm from _____.

3. Now I live in _____.

4. My address is _____.

5. My zip code is _____.

6. My telephone number is _____.

| married | divorced |
| single | widowed |

7. I'm _____.

8. I have _____ children.

9. I have _____ daughters and _____ sons.

10. _____ children are in school.

11. I go to _____ school.

12. My teacher's name is _____.

13. This is my family.

My Family

See the Teacher's Guide.

Sue and Kim have 4 children.
They have 2 sons and 2 daughters.
3 children are in school.
1 child is at home.

1. Do Sue and Kim have children?

   _____.

2. How many children do they have?

   _____.

3. Do they have sons?

   _____.

4. How many sons do they have?

   _____.

5. Do they have daughters?

   _____.

6. How many daughters do they have?

   _____.

7. How many children are in school?

   _____.

8. How many children are at home?

   _____.

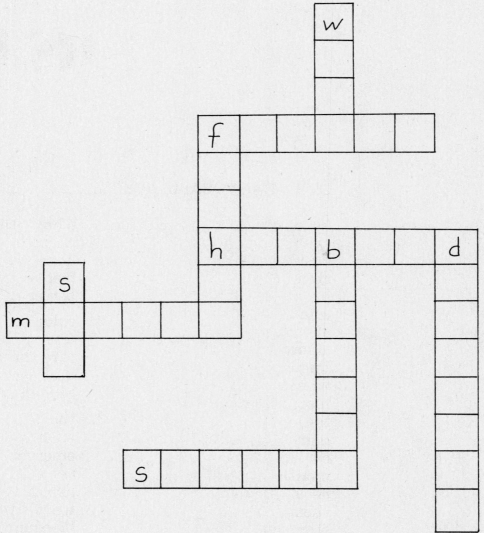

friend
mother
father
husband
wife
son
daughter
brother
sister

HEALTH

ESSENTIAL VOCABULARY ─────────────────

1. head
   eye
   nose
   chin
   back
   arm
   shoulder
   elbow
   finger
   wrist
   foot
   toe
   hair
   ear
   mouth
   neck
   chest
   stomach
   hand
   knee
   leg
   ankle
   body
   sick

   what's the matter
   hurts
   hope
   feel
   better

2. cold
   fever
   sore throat
   a
   broken arm

3. this
   an
   emergency
   need
   doctor
   what's wrong
   bleeding

4. let's take
   temperature
   to see

5. new
   patient

fill out
form
sex
male
female

6. hello
let me see
say
cough
some
medicine
here's
prescription
tablet
night
teaspoon
every
hours
drops
capsules

7. Dr. Paul's
office
this
check up
OK
bye

8. coming
dentist
tooth
when
appointment
next

9. hospital
to visit
new
baby
that's wonderful

10. were
had
that's too bad
wrong

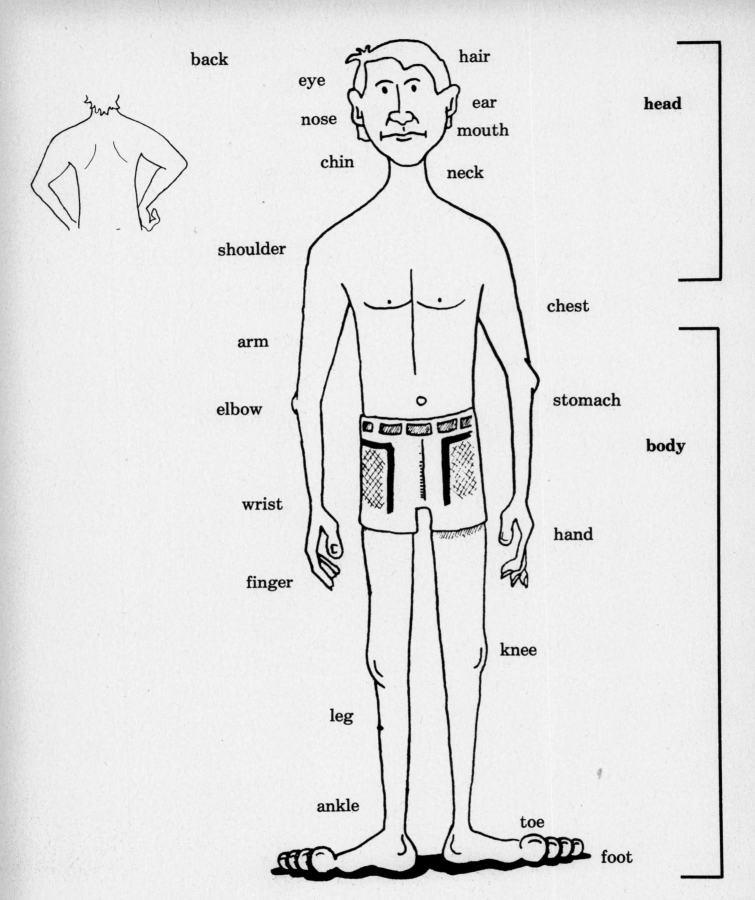

back

hair

eye

ear

nose

mouth

chin

neck

head

shoulder

chest

arm

elbow

stomach

body

wrist

hand

finger

knee

leg

ankle

toe

foot

HEALTH 1

A. How are you?

B. I'm sick.

A. What's the matter?

B. My stomach hurts.

A. I hope you feel better.

Match

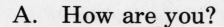

1. eye	11. hair
2. nose	12. ear
3. chin	13. mouth
4. back	14. neck
5. arm	15. chest
6. elbow	16. stomach
7. finger	17. hand
8. foot	18. knee
9. toe	19. leg
10. body	20. head
	21. shoulder

WHAT'S THE MATTER?

 1. My _____ _____.

 2. My _____ _____.

 3. Her _____ _____.

 4. Her _____ _____.

 5. His _____ _____.

 6. His _____ _____.

 7. Their _____ s _____.

 8. Their _____ s _____.

HEALTH 2

First name _____

A. Do you have a cold?
B. Yes, I do.
A. Do you have a fever?
B. No, I don't.

1. They have colds.

2. He has a fever.

3. He has a broken arm.

4. She has a sore throat.

No,	he she	doesn't
	I they	don't

He She	has
I They	have

1. Does he have a fever?

No, _____ _____.

He has _____ _____ _____.

2. Does she have a cold?

No, _____ _____.

_____ _____ _____ _____ _____.

3. Do they have broken arms?

No, _____ _____.

_____ _____ _____ _____.

4. Does he have a sore throat?

No, _____ _____.

_____ _____ _____ _____.

5. Do you have a cold?

_____, I _____.

6. Do you have a fever?

_____, I _____.

7. Do you have a sore throat?

_____, I _____.

90

Lee is sick today.
He has a cold.
He has a sore throat.
He isn't going to school.
He's at home.

1. How is Lee?

   _____.

2. Is he sick?

   _____.

3. What's the matter?

   _____.

4. Does he have a cold?

   _____.

5. Does he have a sore throat?

   _____.

6. Does his stomach hurt?

   _____.

7. Is he going to school?

   _____.

8. Is he at home?

   _____.

calling
going
filling out

coughing
taking
giving

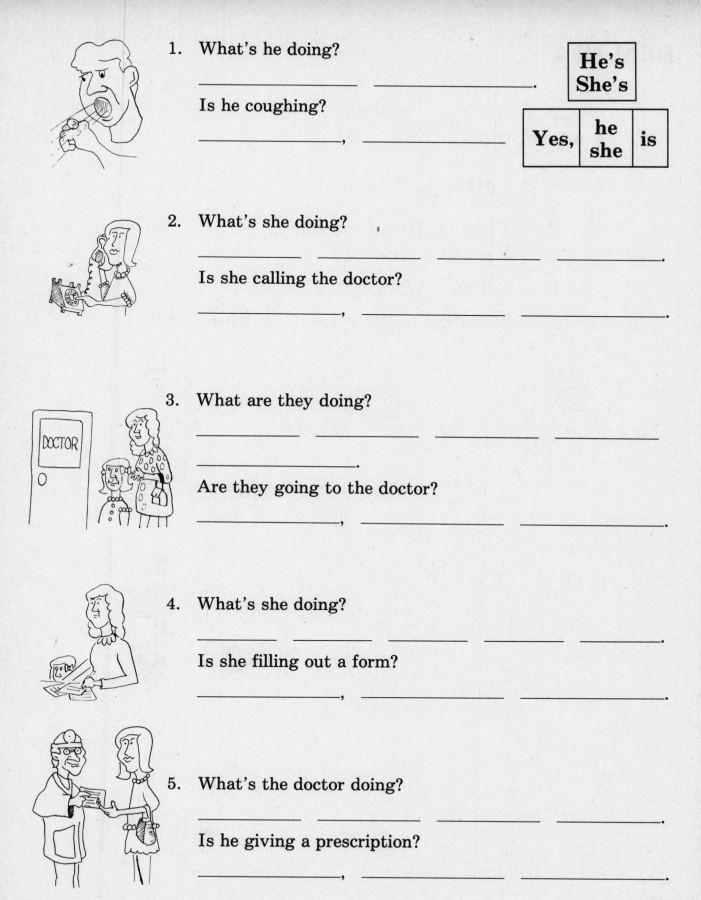

1. What's he doing?

_____ _____ .

Is he coughing?

_____ , _____

He's She's		
Yes,	he she	is

2. What's she doing?

_____ _____ _____ .

Is she calling the doctor?

_____ , _____ _____ .

3. What are they doing?

_____ _____ _____ _____

_____ .

Are they going to the doctor?

_____ , _____ .

4. What's she doing?

_____ _____ _____ .

Is she filling out a form?

_____ , _____ .

5. What's the doctor doing?

_____ _____ _____ .

Is he giving a prescription?

_____ , _____ _____ .

93

HEALTH 3

911

A. This is an emergency.
   I need a doctor.
B. What's wrong?
A. My daughter's head is bleeding.

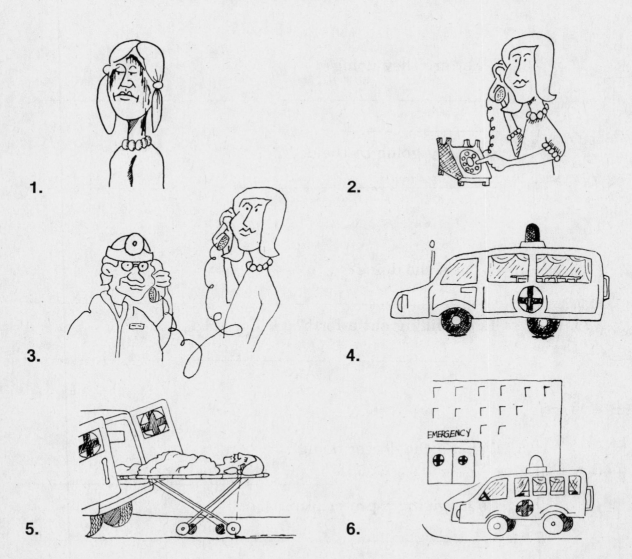

1.

2.

3.

4.

5.

6.

HEALTH 4

Name _____

A. What's wrong?

B. I have a sore throat.

A. Let's take your temperature.
It's 104°.
You need to see a doctor.

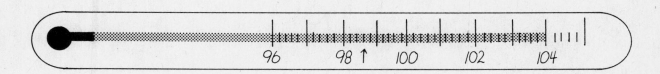

1. It's 104°.

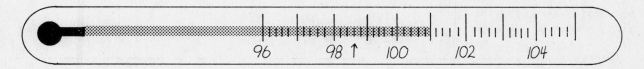

2. It's _____°.

3. It's _____°.

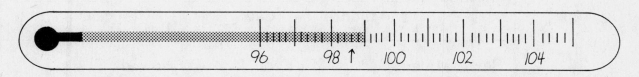

4. It's _____°.

HEALTH 5

Last name _____

A. Are you a new patient?

B. Yes, I am.

A. Please fill out this form.

Name _____
           last   first

Address _____
           number   street

          _____
           city   state   zip code

Phone _____ Age _____

Birthdate _____
             month   day   year

Sex: Male ☐   Married ☐   Widowed ☐
      Female ☐   Single ☐   Divorced ☐

HEALTH 6

A. Hello.
   What's the matter today?

B. I have a sore throat.

A. Let me see.
   Open your mouth.
   Say, "ah."
   Cough.
   You need some medicine.
   Here's a prescription.

Dr. Lee

Name _____ Date _____

Address _____

R
X

_____
doctor's name

1. How much?

   _____

   When?

   _____

2. How much?

   _____

   When?

   _____

tablespoon

3. How much?

   _____

   When?

   _____

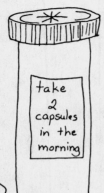

4. How much?

   _____

   When?

   _____

teaspoon

HEALTH 7

First name _____

A. Hello.
Dr. Paul's office.

B. Hello.
This is _____.
My son needs a check up.

A. What's his name?

B. _____.

A. O.K. Come in tomorrow at 3:00.

B. Thanks, bye.

| need |
| needs |

1. I _____ a check up.

2. You _____ a check up.

3. He _____ a check up.

4. She _____ a check up.

5. We _____ a check up.

6. They _____ a check up.

7. Bob _____ a check up.

8. Ann _____ a check up.

WHAT'S THE MATTER?

I	need
he she	needs

1. His head hurts.

   He _____ some medicine.

2. Her back hurts.

   She _____ some medicine.

3. My stomach hurts.

   I _____ some medicine.

medicine

4. My ear hurts.

   I _____ some medicine.

5. His chest hurts.

   He _____ to see a doctor.

6. Her knee hurts.

   She _____ to see a doctor.

7. My shoulder hurts.

   I _____ to see a doctor.

8. My foot hurts.

   I _____ to see a doctor.

doctor

Telephone number _____

A. Teacher, I'm not coming to school tomorrow.

B. What's wrong?

A. I'm going to the dentist.

B. Does your tooth hurt?

A. No, it doesn't.
I need a check up.

B. When is your appointment?

A. At 10:00.

B. O.K.

APPOINTMENT

Ann Lee

Mon. Sep. 18   _10:00_am

Marlow L. Toms D.D.S.
792-4836

NEXT APPOINTMENT

Tue. Jan 4   _4:30_ p.m.

Bob Jones

Dr. B. E. White
876-6927

---

1. What date is the appointment?

   _____.

2. What time is the appointment?

   _____.

3. What date is the appointment?

   _____.

4. What time is the appointment?

   _____.

Zip code _____

A. Teacher, I'm not coming to school tomorrow.

B. Why?

A. Because I'm going to the hospital to visit my friend.

B. Is she sick?

A. No, she isn't.
    She has a new baby.

B. That's wonderful.

Draw a Person

See the Teacher's Guide.

HEALTH 10

State _____

A. Were you sick yesterday?

B. Yes, I was.

A. What was wrong?

B. I had a cold.

A. That's too bad.

I He She	was	sick
We You They	were	

I'm He's She's We're You're They're	fine

YESTERDAY

1. I ___was___ sick.

2. He _____ _____ .

3. She _____ _____ .

4. We _____ _____ .

5. You _____ _____ .

6. They _____ _____ .

TODAY

1. ___I'm___ fine.

2. _____ _____ .

3. _____ _____ .

4. _____ _____ .

5. _____ _____ .

6. _____ _____ .

1. Bob is sick.
   He has a fever.

2. His mother calls the doctor.

3. Bob and his mother go to the doctor.

4. The nurse takes Bob's temperature.

5. The doctor gives Bob a prescription.

The nurse takes Bob's temperature.

_ _

His mother calls the doctor.

_ _

Bob is sick. He has a fever.

_ _

Bob and his mother go to the doctor.

_ _

The doctor gives Bob a prescription.

_ _

See the Teacher's Guide.

Tran was sick yesterday.
He wasn't at school.
He had a sore throat.

1. Who was sick yesterday?

    _____.

2. Was Tran sick yesterday?

    _____.

3. Was Tran at home yesterday?

    _____.

4. Was Tran at school yesterday?

    _____.

5. What was wrong?

    _____.

6. Why was Tran home?

    _____.

7. Were you sick yesterday?

    _____.

8. Were you at school yesterday?

    _____.

9. Were you at home yesterday?

    _____.

finger ear mouth stomach toes arm shoulders back chest hair elbow nose foot head eye knee hand leg

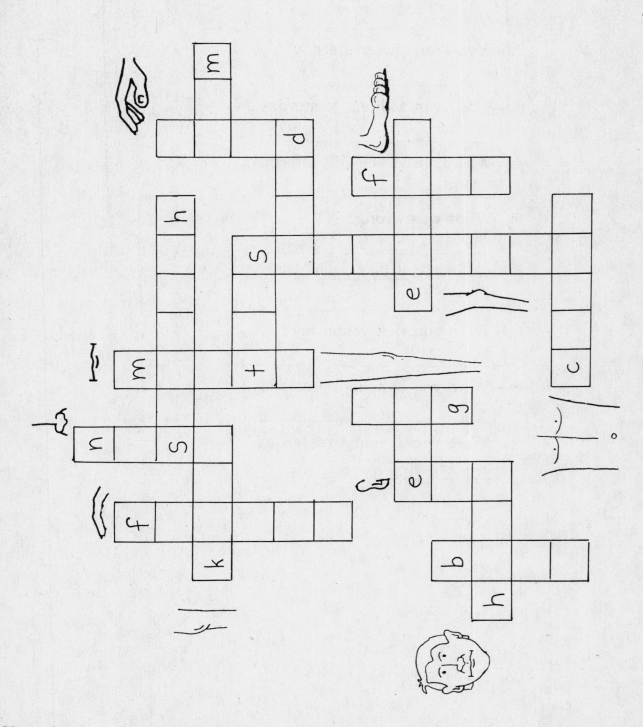

5

TRANSPORTATION

ESSENTIAL VOCABULARY

1. drive
   take
   train
   ride

2. Bus Company
   downtown
   to transfer
   every hour

3. bus stop
   over there
   in front of
   in back of
   next to
   gas station

4. how much
   one way

5. watch your step
   be careful

6. grocery store
   First Street
   on the corner
   pharmacy

7. lost
   shopping center
   turn left
   turn right
   block

8. driver's license
   I'm sorry

9. too fast
   speed limit
   giving
   ticket

10. mechanic
    check
    car
    sure
    engine
    battery
    radiator
    just
    water

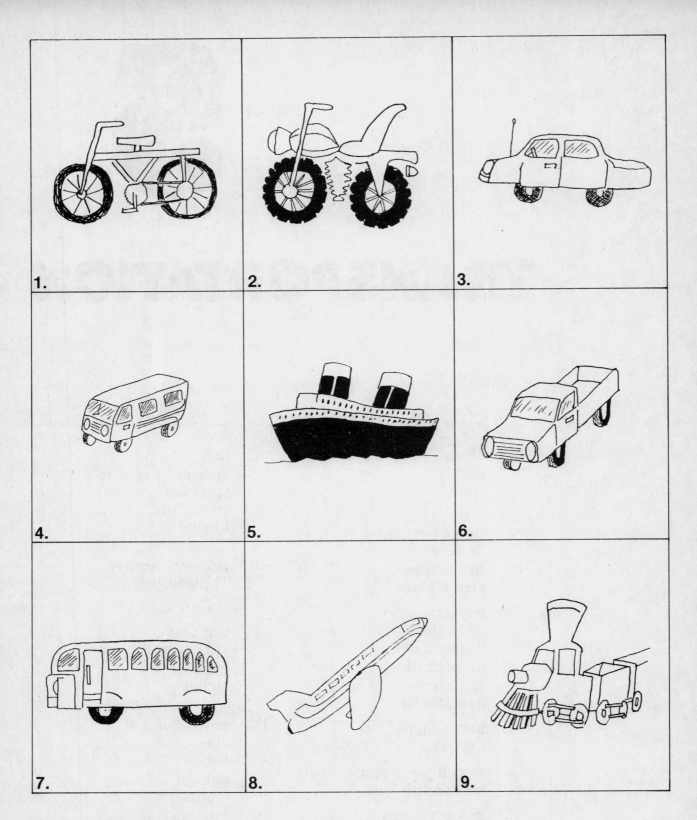

bicycle
van
bus

motorcycle
boat
airplane

car
truck
train

TRANSPORTATION 1

City _____

A. I drive to school.
   How do you go to school?

B. I take the bus.

I drive a

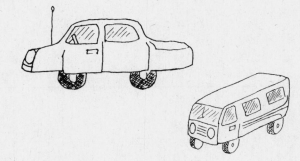

I ride a

to school.

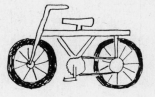

I take the

How does 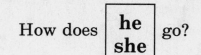 go?

She walks.
He drives his car.
She takes the bus.

He rides his bicycle.
He takes the train.
She takes an airplane.

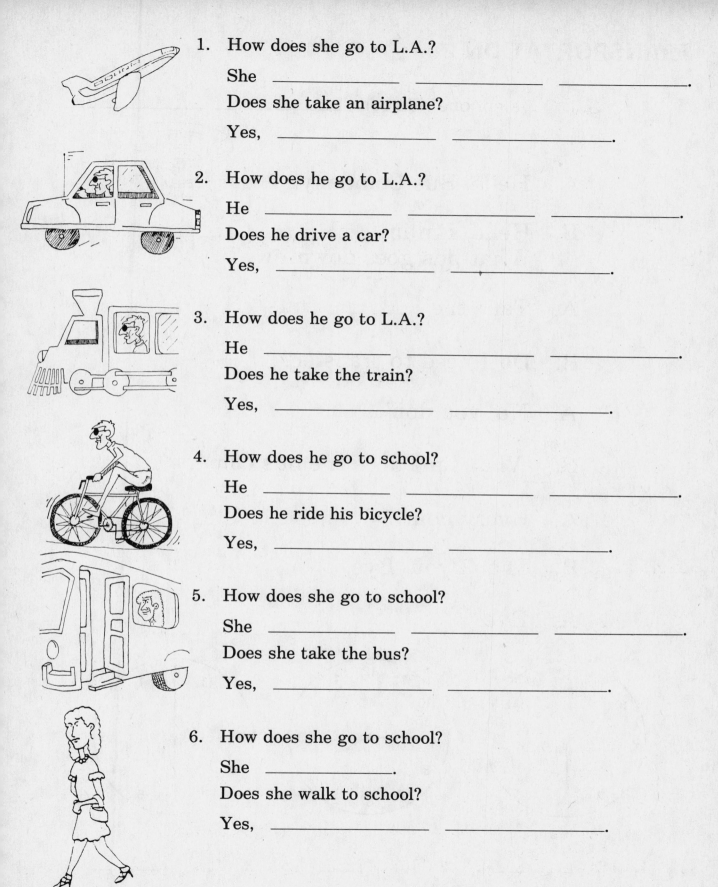

1. How does she go to L.A.?

   She _____ _____ _____.

   Does she take an airplane?

   Yes, _____ _____.

2. How does he go to L.A.?

   He _____ _____ _____.

   Does he drive a car?

   Yes, _____ _____.

3. How does he go to L.A.?

   He _____ _____ _____.

   Does he take the train?

   Yes, _____ _____.

4. How does he go to school?

   He _____ _____ _____.

   Does he ride his bicycle?

   Yes, _____ _____.

5. How does she go to school?

   She _____ _____ _____.

   Does she take the bus?

   Yes, _____ _____.

6. How does she go to school?

   She _____.

   Does she walk to school?

   Yes, _____ _____.

TRANSPORTATION 2

Telephone number _____

A. Hello, Bus Company.

B. Hello, I'm in _____.
What bus goes downtown?

A. Take the _____ bus.

B. Do I need to transfer?

A. No, you don't.

B. What time does the bus come?

A. Every hour.

B. Thank you. Bye.

A. Bye.

  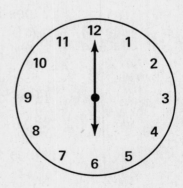

1. It's _____. 2. It's _____. 3. It's _____.

Who?	How do they come to school? / How does he / she come to school?	How do they go downtown? / How does he / she go downtown?
Bob		
Ann		
They		

downtown
grocery store
laundromat
shopping center

hospital
home
park
theater

school
church
pharmacy
gas station

TRANSPORTATION 3

Social security number _____

A. Where's the bus stop?

B. It's over there.

It's | in front of | the gas station.

| in front of |
| in back of |
| next to |

Match

gas station

theater

grocery store

hospital

church

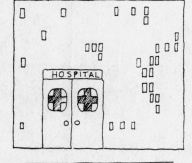

laundromat

pharmacy

shopping center

TRANSPORTATION 4

Birth date _____

A. Where are you going?

B. I'm going downtown.

A. Are you taking the bus?

B. Yes, I am.

A. How much is it?

B. _____ one way.

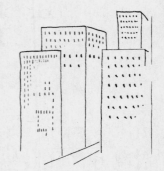

I'm going  _____.

I'm going to  _____.

I'm going to the  _____.

TRANSPORTATION 5

Age _____

A. Is this bus going downtown?
B. Yes, it is. Watch your step. Be careful.
A. Do I need to transfer?
B. No, you don't.
A. Thanks.

Do	I you we they	___ ?

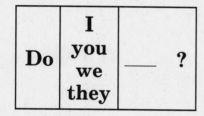

Does	he she	___ ?

1. _____ I need to transfer?
2. _____ they need to transfer?
3. _____ we need to transfer?
4. _____ she need to _____?
5. _____ he need to _____?
6. _____ I need _____ _____?
7. _____ you need _____ _____?
8. _____ they _____ _____ _____?
9. _____ she _____ _____ _____?
10. _____ he _____ _____ _____?

Where's the _____ going?

1. The _____ is going _____.

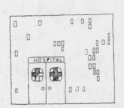

2. The _____ is going to the _____.

3. The _____ is going to the _____ _____.

118

1.

3.

5.

7.

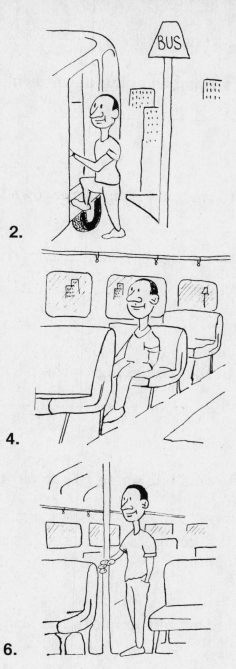

2.

4.

6.

1. Wait for the bus.
2. Get on.
3. Pay the fare.
4. Sit down.
5. Pull the bell.
6. Stand up.
7. Get off.

1. Is this bus going downtown?

   _____, _____ _____.

2. Is this bus going downtown?

   _____, _____ _____.

   It's going _____ _____ _____.

3. Is this bus going to the park?

   _____, _____ _____.

4. Is this bus going to the park?

   _____, _____ _____.

   It's going _____.

5. Is this bus going to the shopping
   center?

   _____, _____ _____.

6. Is this bus going to the hospital?

   _____, _____ _____.

   It's going _____ _____ _____.

TRANSPORTATION 6

Date _____

A. Excuse me. Where's the grocery store?
B. It's on First Street.
A. Is it on the corner?
B. No, it isn't. It's next to the pharmacy.
A. Thank you.

Where's the _____? It's

next to in front of	the _____.
on the corner.	

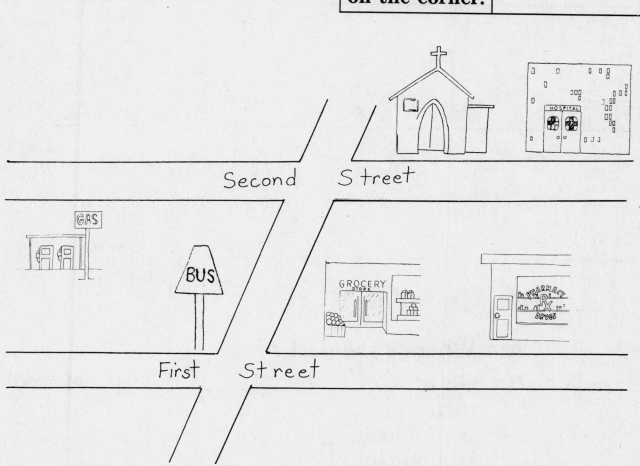

Name _____

A.   I'm lost. Where's the shopping center?

B.   Go to A Street and turn right.
Turn left on First Street.
Turn right on B Street.
It's on the corner.

A.   Thanks.

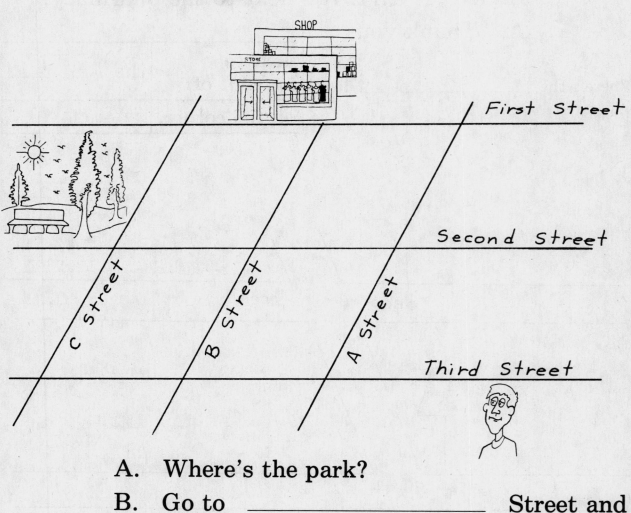

A.   Where's the park?

B.   Go to _____ Street and
turn _____ .
Go 1 block.
It's on the _____ .

MAP

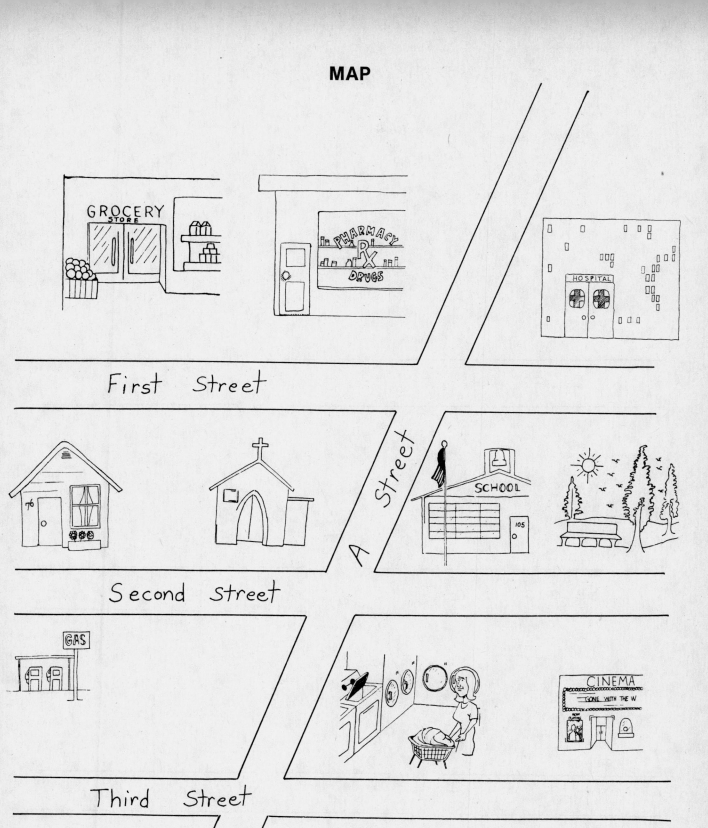

See the Teacher's Guide.

MAP

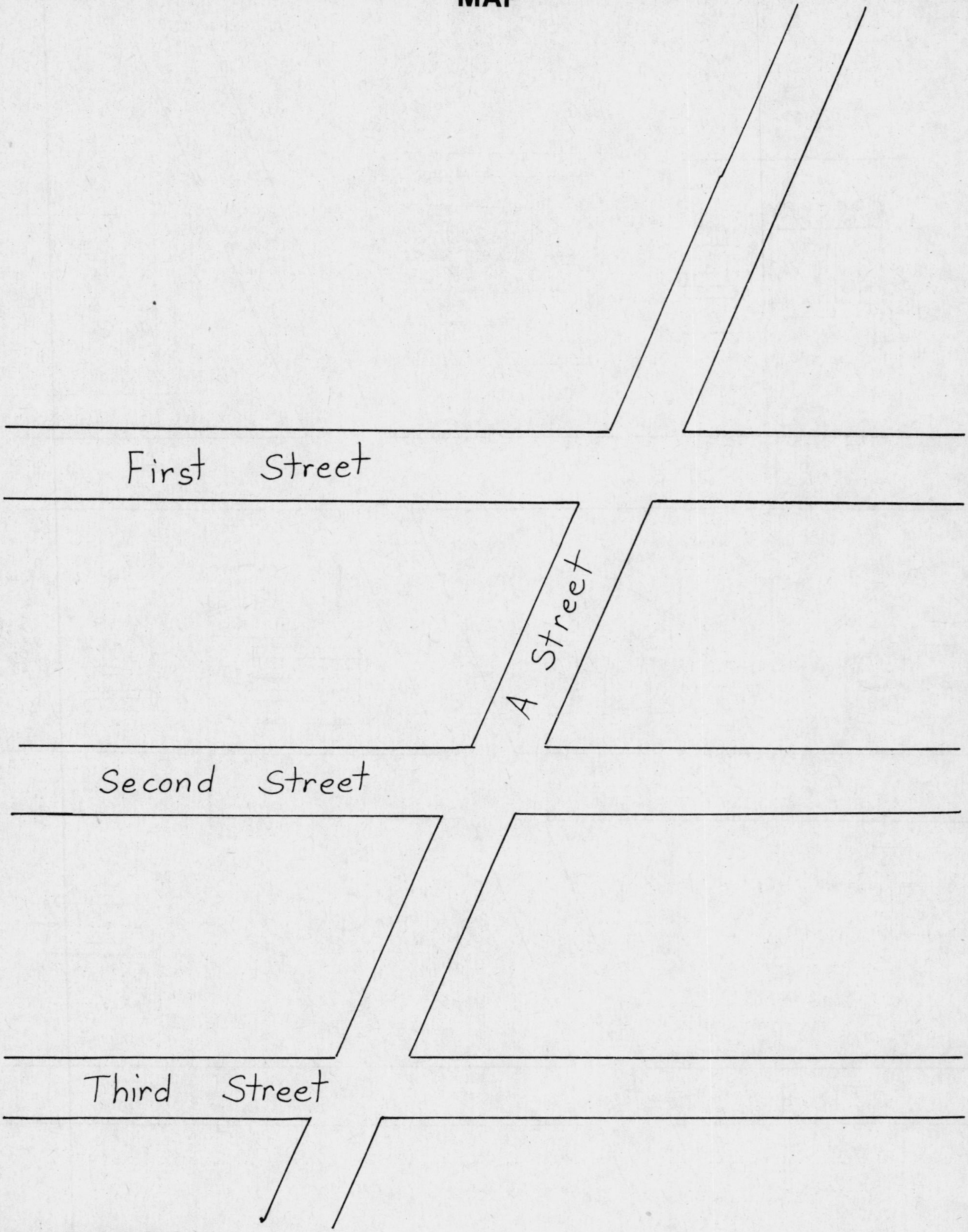

First Street

A Street

Second Street

Third Street

See the Teacher's Guide.

1. **Where's the pharmacy?**
   _____ _____ on _____ First _____ Street.

   Is it on the corner?

   _____, _____ _____.

2. **Where's the laundromat?**
   It's _____ _____.

   Is it on the corner?

   _____, _____ _____.

3. **Where's the church?**
   It's _____ _____.

   Is it on the corner?

   _____, _____ _____.

4. **Where's the park?**
   It's _____ _____.

   Is it on the corner?

   _____, _____ _____.

5. **Where's the grocery store?**
   It's _____ _____.

   Is it on the corner?

   _____, _____ _____.

6. **Where's the hospital?**
   It's _____ _____.

   Is it on the corner?

   _____, _____.

Who?	Where?	How?

See the Teacher's Guide.

TRANSPORTATION 8

First name _____

A. Do you have a driver's license?

B. No, I don't.

A. That's too bad.
   You need a driver's license.

B. Oh, I'm sorry.

A. Don't drive.

B. Don't drive?

A. Don't drive!

B. O.K.

 Don't turn left.

 No left turn.

 Don't turn right.

 No right turn.

 Don't make a U-turn.

 Don't walk.

No walking.

 No U-turn.

Mary is going to a movie.
The theater is downtown.
She takes the #10 bus.
She doesn't need to transfer.
The fare is 80¢ one way.

1. Who's going to the movie?

_____

2. Where's Mary going?

_____

3. Where's the theater?

_____

4. Is Mary going to a movie?

_____

5. Is Mary going downtown?

_____

6. Is Mary taking the bus?

_____

7. Is Mary driving a car?

_____

8. What bus goes downtown?

_____

9. How much is the fare one way?

_____

10. How much is the fare round trip?

_____

TRANSPORTATION 9

Last name _____

A. Do you have a driver's license?

B. Yes, I do. What's the matter?

A. You were driving too fast. The speed limit is 55, not 65.

B. I'm sorry.

A. I'm giving you a ticket.

Address _____

A. Are you a mechanic?
B. Yes, I am.

A. Can you check my car?
B. Sure.

A. How's the engine?
B. It's OK.

A. How's the battery?
B. It's OK.

A. How's the radiator?
B. It just needs some water.
A. Oh, good. Thanks.

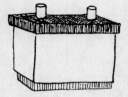

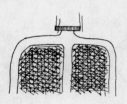

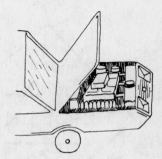

1. _____   2. _____   3. _____   4. _____

131

FOOD

ESSENTIAL VOCABULARY

1. bread
   and
   eggs
   milk
   ice cream

2. hot dogs
   hamburger
   buy some
   pound
   one sale

3. broccoli
   celery
   onions
   pineapple
   pears
   oranges
   mushrooms
   bananas
   grapes
   ea.
   lb.

4. to return
   meat
   fresh
   you're right
   receipt

5. hungry
   let's eat
   like

6. to make
   cake
   cake mix
   cup
   oil
   turn on
   oven
   grease
   pan
   flour
   put
   mix
   bowl
   add
   stir
   wait
   minutes

7. next
   colas
   small
   medium
   large
   to go

bread	hot dog
eggs	a hamburger
milk	soda pop
ice cream	coffee

fish	rice
chicken	oil
pork	tea
hamburger	cake mix

FOOD 1

Zip code _____

A. I'm going to the store.
What do you need?

B. I need bread and eggs.

A. Do you need milk?

B. No, I don't. I have milk.

A. Do you want ice cream?

B. No, I don't.

	have — has	need — needs
I You They We		
He She		

1. I don't have and .

   I need _____ and _____ .

2. I don't have and .

   I need _____ and _____ .

3. He doesn't have and .

   He needs _____ and _____ .

4. He doesn't have and .

   He needs _____ and _____ .

5. She doesn't have and .

   She needs _____ and _____ .

6. She doesn't have and .

   She needs _____ and _____ .

FOOD 2

pound — lb.

A. Do you like hot dogs?
B. No, I don't.
A. Do you like hamburger?
B. Yes, I do. I want to buy some.
A. It's $1.09 a pound on sale.

Hamburger		
Per Lb. 1.39	Total 4.17	Wt. 3
J.G's Market		

How much is it a pound?

_____

What's the total?

_____

Pork		
Total 4.47	Per Lb. 1.49	Wt. 3

1. How much is it a pound?

_____

2. What's the total?

_____

Fish Market		
Wt. 3.96	Total 4.95	Per Lb. 1.25
Fish		

3. How much is it a pound?

_____

4. What's the total?

_____

Hamburger		
Per Lb. .96	Total 3.40	Wt. 3.54

5. How much is it a pound?

_____

6. What's the total?

_____

Quacky Farms		
Per Lb. .49	Wt. 5.62	Total 2.75
Chicken		

7. How much is it a pound?

_____

8. What's the total?

_____

1.

2.

3.

4.

5.

6.

7.

8.

9.

10.

11.

12.

13.

14.

15.

16.

17.

18.

pineapple
apples
oranges

bananas
grapes
pears

broccoli
celery
onions

squash
potatoes
tomatoes

mushrooms
carrots
peppers

corn
peas
beans

1. Does he like _____ ?

   Yes, _____ _____ .

2. Does he like _____ ?

   No, _____ _____ .

3. Do they like _____ ?

   Yes, _____ _____ .

4. Do they like _____ ?

   No, _____ _____ .

5. Does she like _____ ?

   Yes, _____ _____ .

6. Does she like _____ ?

   No, _____ _____ .

7. Do you like _____ ?

   _____ , _____ _____ .

8. Do you like _____ ?

   _____ , _____ _____ .

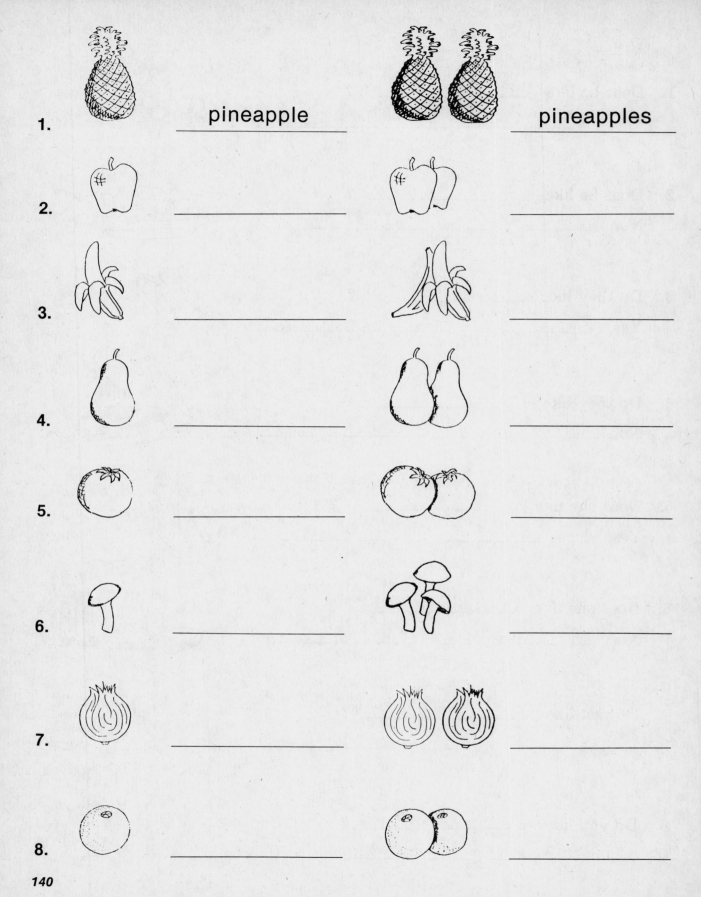

1. pineapple _____   pineapples _____

2. _____   _____

3. _____   _____

4. _____   _____

5. _____   _____

6. _____   _____

7. _____   _____

8. _____   _____

1. <u>He's</u> <u>going</u> to the store. <u>He</u> <u>needs</u> <u>bananas.</u>

2. _____ _____ to the store. _____ _____ apples.

3. _____ _____ to the store. _____ _____ milk.

4. _____ _____ to the store. _____ _____ oranges.

5. _____ _____ to the store. _____ _____ pears.

6. _____ _____ to the store. _____ _____ squash.

7. _____ _____ to the store. _____ _____ broccoli.

8. _____ _____ to the store. _____ _____ celery.

FOOD 3

City _____

A. How much is the ?

B. 49¢ a lb.

A. How much is the ?

B. 52¢ ea.

A. How much are the ?

B. 32¢ a lb.

A. How much is the ?

B. $3.10 ea.

69¢ a lb.

33¢ a lb.

49¢ a lb.

$1.98 ½ lb.

87¢ a lb.

33¢ a lb.

pears _____   oranges _____   pineapple _____

grapes _____   bananas _____   mushrooms _____

onions _____   broccoli _____   celery _____

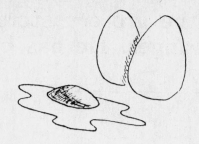

81¢ a doz.

$1.02

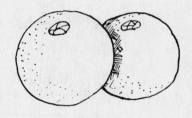

$2.17

78¢

1. How much is the fish?

It's _____.

2. How much is the milk?

It's _____.

3. How much are the eggs?

They're _____.

4. How much are the oranges?

They're _____.

5. How much are the fish and eggs?

_____ _____.

6. How much are the milk and eggs?

_____ _____.

7. How much are the oranges and fish?

_____ _____.

8. How much are the eggs, milk, and oranges?

_____ _____.

Keo is going to the grocery store. He needs eggs, rice, and oranges. He has bananas and milk.

1. Who's going to the grocery store?

   _____.

2. Where's Keo going?

   _____.

3. Is he going to the grocery store?

   _____.

4. What does Keo need?

   _____.

5. What does Keo have?

   _____.

6. Does Keo need eggs?

   _____.

7. Does Keo need rice?

   _____.

8. Does Keo need milk?

   _____.

9. Does Keo have bananas?

   _____.

10. Does Keo have milk?

   _____.

11. Does Keo need bananas?

   _____.

FOOD 4

Telephone number _____

A. Excuse me. I want to return this meat.
B. Why?
A. Because it isn't fresh.
B. Let me see. Oh! You're right.
   Do you have the receipt?
A. Yes, I do.

Hamburger		
Total $2.00	Per Lb. $1.00	Wt. 2
JUL 06		

Today is July 6.
1. What's the date on the meat?

   _____.

2. Is it fresh?

   _____, _____ _____.

Today is November 15.
3. What's the date on the milk?

   _____.

4. Is it fresh?

   _____, _____ _____.

1. 2.

3. 4.

5. 6.

eating   drinking
returning   making/cooking
shopping   buying

1. What's he doing?

_____ _____.

Is he eating?

_____, _____ _____.

2. What's she doing?

_____ _____.

Is she shopping?

_____, _____ _____.

3. What's he doing?

_____ _____.

Is he eating?

_____, _____ _____.

4. What's she doing?

_____ _____ meat.

Is she cooking?

_____, _____ _____.

5. What's he doing?

_____ _____.

Is he drinking?

_____, _____ _____.

6. What's she doing?

_____ _____ food.

Is she returning meat?

_____, _____ _____.

FOOD 5

A. I'm hungry.
B. I'm hungry, too.

A. Let's eat some _____.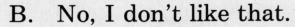
B. No, I don't like that.

A. OK. Let's eat some _____.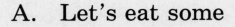
B. OK. I like that.

He's hungry.
He's eating a hot dog.

He's thirsty.
He's drinking.

148

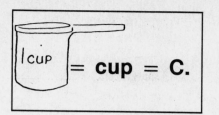

1 cup = **cup** = **C.**

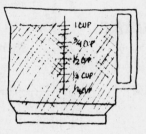

1C

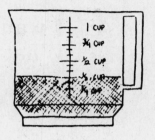

⅓ C

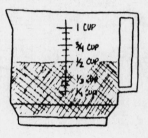

½ C

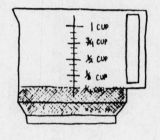

¼ C

Fill-in

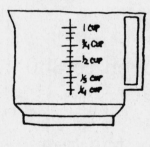

⅓ C

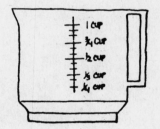

1C

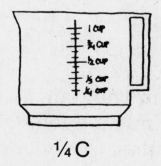

¼ C

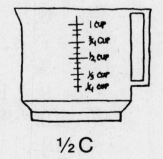

½ C

FOOD 6

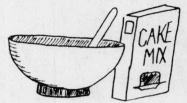

A. I want to make a cake.
What do I need?

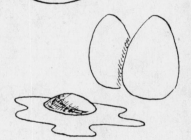

B. You need a cake mix
        $1\frac{1}{2}$ cups water
        $\frac{1}{3}$ cup oil
        and 3 eggs.

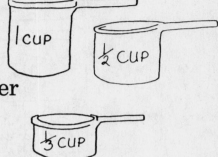

A. Do you want to help?
B. Sure.

A.   1. Turn on the oven to 350°.
       2. Grease the pan.
       3. Flour the pan.
       4. Put the mix in the bowl.
       5. Add the water.
       6. Add the eggs.
       7. Add the oil.
       8. Stir it up.
       9. Put the mix in the pan.
      10. Put the pan in the oven.
      11. Wait 35 minutes.

Powdered Milk

1⅓ C powdered milk mix

4 C water

mix

1. How much water? _____

2. How much powdered milk mix? _____

Hamburger Casserole

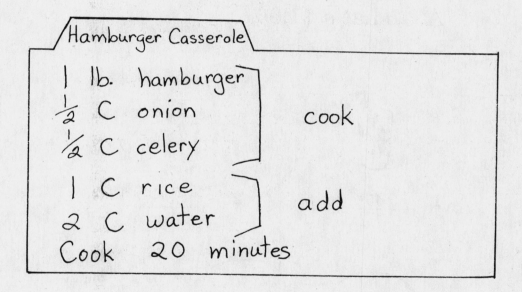

1 lb. hamburger
½ C onion   } cook
½ C celery

1 C rice   } add
2 C water

Cook 20 minutes

3. How much water? _____

4. How much onion? _____

5. How much hamburger? _____

6. How much celery? _____

7. How much rice? _____

FOOD 7

A. Next, please.

B. I want two colas.

A. Small, medium, or large?

B. One small, one medium.

A. Is that for here or to go?

B. To go.

A. That's $1.00.

1. _____45¢_____   2. _____55¢_____   3. _____65¢_____

4. _____65¢_____ 5. _____95¢_____ 6. ___60¢___ 7. ___90¢___

Julia cooks every day. Today she opens the hamburger. It isn't fresh. She needs fresh hamburger. She wants to return the hamburger. She has the receipt. She's going to the grocery store now.

1. Who cooks every day?

   _____

2. Is the hamburger fresh?

   _____

3. Does she need fresh hamburger?

   _____

4. Does she want to return it?

   _____

5. Does she have the receipt?

   _____

6. Where is Julia going now?

   _____

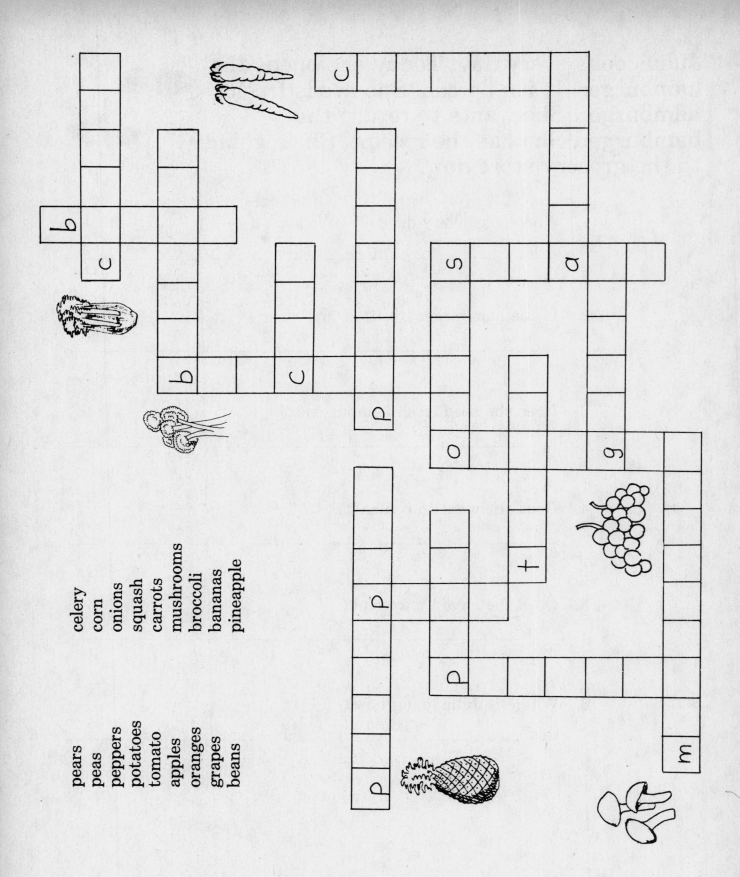

pears
peas
peppers
potatoes
tomato
apples
oranges
grapes
beans

celery
corn
onions
squash
carrots
mushrooms
broccoli
bananas
pineapple

7

CLOTHING

ESSENTIAL VOCABULARY _____

1. look nice
   dress
   beautiful

2. jackets
   for
   pants
   socks
   belts
   shoes
   dresses
   shirts
   hats
   sweaters

3. try it on
   too small
   too big
   just right
   let's buy it
   size

4. on sale
   I'll buy it

5. color
   brown
   exchange
   red
   black
   yellow
   green
   blue

6. Can I help you?

7. cash
   or
   charge
   let's see
   plus
   tax
   money
   change
   from

8. outside
   just a minute
   pull up

tie
now
button
put on
zip

9. sewing class
free
making
difficult
easy
fun

10. pick up
thread

scissors
cut
needle
knot
material
sew
up
down

11. laundromat
clothes
to wash
soap
bleach
machines

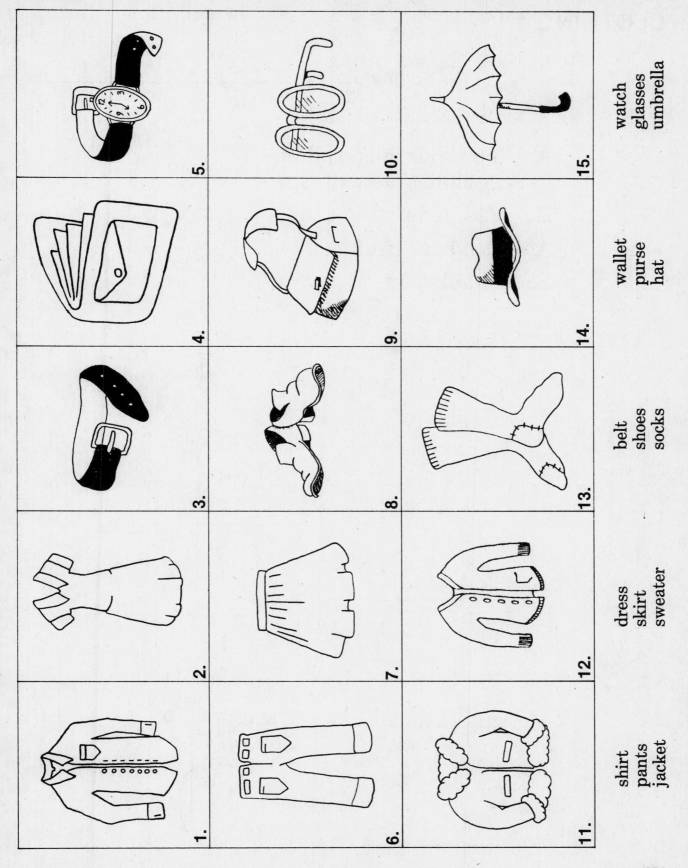

shirt pants jacket	dress skirt sweater	belt shoes socks	wallet purse hat	watch glasses umbrella

1. 2. 3. 4. 5.

6. 7. 8. 9. 10.

11. 12. 13. 14. 15.

157

CLOTHING 1

A. You look nice today.
   Is that a new dress?
B. Yes, it is.
A. It's beautiful.
B. Thank you.

1. _____

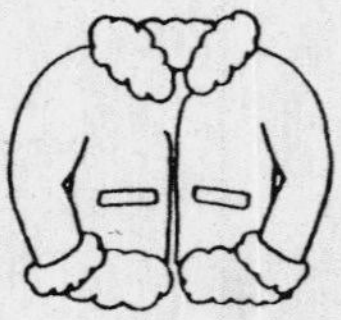

2. _____

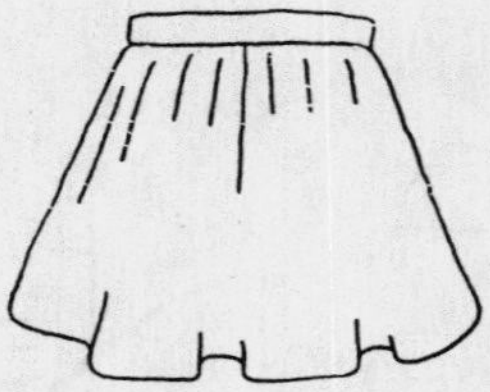

3. _____

4. _____

5. _____

6. _____

7. _____

8. _____

9. _____

10. _____

CLOTHING 2

A. I'm going to the shopping center.

B. When?

A. At 2:00. Do you want to come?

B. Yes, I do. I need to buy jackets for my children.

1. I   need   to   buy   _____.

2. I   need   _____ _____ _____.

3. I   need   _____ _____ a   _____.

4. I   need   _____ _____ an   _____.

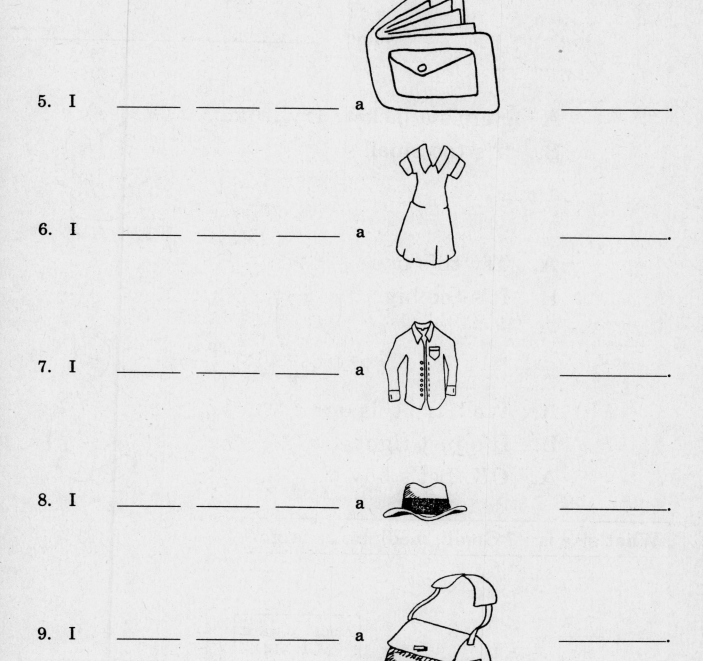

5. I _____ _____ _____ a _____.

6. I _____ _____ _____ a _____.

7. I _____ _____ _____ a _____.

8. I _____ _____ _____ a _____.

9. I _____ _____ _____ a _____.

CLOTHING 3

Name 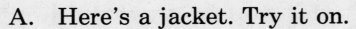 _____

A. Here's a jacket. Try it on.
B. It's too small.

A. Try this one.
B. It's too big.

A. Well, try this one.
B. It's just right.
A. OK. Let's buy it.

What size is it? Small, medium, or large?

| sm. | 1. _____ | machine wash M 12–14 | 2. _____ |

| lg. | 3. _____ | L 14–16 | 4. _____ |

| m | 5. _____ | s | 6. _____ | L | 7. _____ |

CLOTHING 4

First name _____

A. I like this dress.
   How much is it?
B. Now it's $12.00 on sale.
A. On sale?
B. Yes, it was $16.00.
A. I'll buy it.

was	on sale
$19.95	$14.95
$8.95	$5.20
$24.99	$18.59
$10.00	$6.99

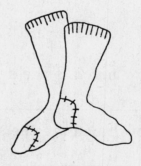

were	on sale
$17.00	$12.99
$2.00	$1.49
$8.50	$5.99

ON SALE

$5.99

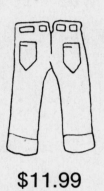

$8.49

$6.00

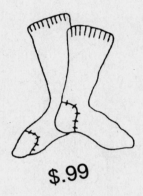

$.99

$11.99

$5.00

1. How much is the sweater?

_____ _____.

2. How much are the socks?

_____ _____.

3. How much is the skirt?

_____ _____.

4. How much are the pants?

_____ _____.

5. How much is the shirt?

_____ _____.

6. How much are the shoes?

_____ _____.

1.	2.	3.
4.	5.	6.
7.	8.	9.

1. Color number 1 red.

2. Color number 2 green.

3. Color number 3 yellow.

4. Color number 4 orange.

5. Color number 5 blue.

6. Color number 6 purple.

7. Color number 7 brown.

8. Color number 8 black.

9. Don't color number 9. It's white.

See the Teacher's Guide.

Ann needs to buy jackets for her children. She needs 1 small and 1 large jacket. The children want blue jackets. Ann wants to buy the jackets on sale.

1. Does Ann need jackets for her children?

   _____.

2. How many jackets does she need?

   _____.

3. What colors?

   _____.

4. What sizes?

   _____.

5. Does she want to buy the jackets on sale?

   _____.

6. Do the children want blue jackets?

   _____.

7. Do the children want yellow jackets?

   _____.

8. Do you have a jacket?

   _____.

9. What color is it?

   _____.

10. What size is it?

   _____.

CLOTHING 5

Last name _____

A. I have a new dress. Do you like it?

B. No, I don't.

A. Why?

B. Because I don't like the color.
   I don't like brown.

A. Oh, I'll exchange it.

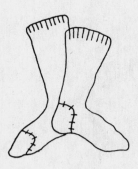

Color the dress red.   Color the skirt yellow.
Color the pants brown.   Color the socks green.
Color the hat black.   Color the shirt blue.

1.

2.

3.

4.

5.

6.

exchanging
sewing
making

washing
trying on
wearing

he	he's
she	she's

1. What's _____ doing?

_____ _____ _____ _____.

2. What's _____ wearing?

_____ _____ _____ _____.

3. What's _____ doing?

_____ _____ _____ _____.

4. What's _____ doing?

_____ _____.

5. What's _____ doing?

_____ _____ _____ _____.

6. What's _____ doing?

_____ _____.

CLOTHING 6

A. Can I help you?

B. Yes, I want to exchange this dress. I want a blue one.

A. Do you have the receipt?

B. Yes, I do.

A.	Can I help you?	What's wrong?	Do you have the receipt?
B.	I want to exchange this _____	too small	yes
		too big	no

CLOTHING 7

Address _____

A. I want to buy this shirt.

B. Cash or charge?

A. Cash.

B. Let's see. $10.00 plus tax.
That's _____.

A. Here's the money.

B. _____ from $11.00. Your
change is _____.

Cash or charge?

1. _____

2. _____

3. _____

4. _____

CLOTHING 8

jacket	shirt	socks	hat	shoes

A. Can I go outside?

B. Just a minute.
   Pull up your _____,
   and tie your _____.

A. OK. Can I go now?

B. Just a minute.
   Button your _____,
   and put on a _____.

A. OK. Can I go now?

B. Just a minute.
   Put on a _____
   and zip it up.

A. Can I go now?

B. Yes, you can.

CLOTHING 9

State _____

A. Where are you going?
B. I'm going to sewing class.

A. How much is it?
B. It's free.

A. What are you making?
B. I'm making a shirt.

A. Is it difficult?
B. No, it isn't. It's easy.

A. Is it fun?
B. Yes, it is.

Ann _____ _____ to sewing class.
She _____ _____ a shirt.

City _____

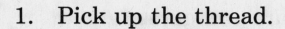

1. Pick up the thread.

2. Pick up the scissors.

3. Cut the thread.

4. Pick up the needle.

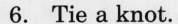

5. Thread the needle.

6. Tie a knot.

7. Put the button on the material.

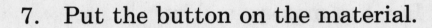

8. Sew the button on the material.

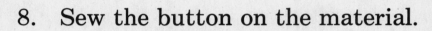

9. Sew up and down, up and down.

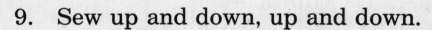

10. Tie a knot.

11. Cut the thread.

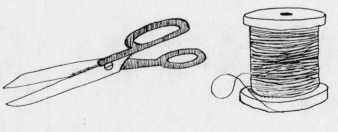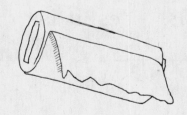

1. _____ 2. _____ 3. _____ 4. _____

5. _____ 6. _____

CLOTHING 11

Telephone number _____

A. Where are you going?

B. I'm going to the laundromat.
   I need to wash my clothes.

A. Do you have soap?

B. Yes, I do.

A. Do you have bleach?

B. No, I don't. I don't need bleach.

A. Do you have change for the machines?

B. Yes, I do.

Ann _____ _____ to the laundromat. She _____ to wash her clothes. She _____ soap. She _____ change for the machines.

175

dress
hat
watch
sweater
belt
socks
shoes
purse
pants
jacket
shirt
skirt
glasses
umbrella

176

8

HOUSING

ESSENTIAL VOCABULARY

1. bedroom

2. live
   house
   apartment
   upstairs
   downstairs

3. busy
   looking for
   people

4. rent
   a month
   furnished
   unfurnished

5. pay
   utilities
   gas
   electricity

6. cleaning deposit
   week

7. call
   manager

   fix
   refrigerator
   mirror
   stove
   broken

8. bathroom
   sink
   leaking

9. borrow
   plunger
   toilet
   stopped up
   screwdriver
   wrench
   hammer
   pliers

10. problem
    cockroaches
    spray
    away

11. moving
    cleaning

Furnished

1. bedroom

2. bathroom

3. living room

4. kitchen

HOUSING 1

Social security number _____

A. Hello.

B. Hello. Is Ann home?

A. Yes, she is. She's in the bedroom. Just a minute.

B. Thanks.

A. Ann, it's for you.

1. She's in the  _____.

2. She's in the 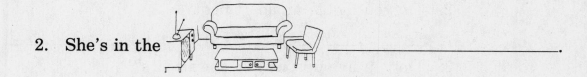 _____.

3. She's in the 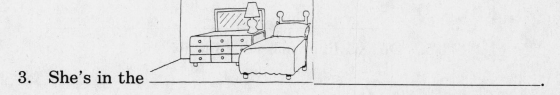 _____.

HOUSING 2

Birth date _____

A. Do you live in a house?
B. No, I don't.
   I live in an apartment.
A. Do you live upstairs or downstairs?
B. I live upstairs.

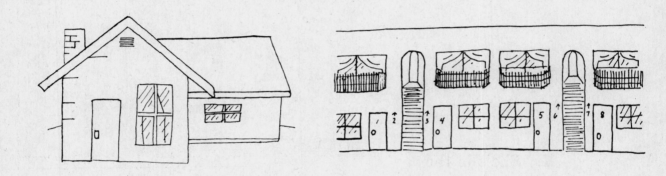

1. Do you live in a house?

   _____.

2. Do you live in an apartment?

   _____.

3. Do you live upstairs or downstairs?

   _____.

4. What's your address?

   _____.

5. Do you live with your family?

   _____.

fixing
cleaning
thinking

looking
moving
borrowing

HOUSING 3

Age _____

A. Hello. How are you?

B. I'm busy. I'm looking for a new apartment.

A. What's the matter?

B. My apartment is too small.
I have 12 people in my family.
I have 1 bedroom.
I need 3 bedrooms.

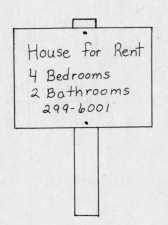

House for Rent
4 Bedrooms
2 Bathrooms
299-6001

1. Is it a house?

   _____

2. How many bedrooms?

   _____

3. How many bathrooms?

   _____

4. What's the telephone number?

   _____

1.

2.

3.

4.

5.

6.

7.

8.

9.

10.

11.

12.

chair	lamp	bed
rug	sink	T.V.
toilet	stove	table
refrigerator	bathtub	sofa

HOUSING 4

A. I need a 3 bedroom apartment. Do you have one?

B. Yes, I do.

A. How much is the rent?

B. It's $400 a month.

A. Is it furnished?

B. No, it isn't. It's unfurnished.

A. Thanks.

Match

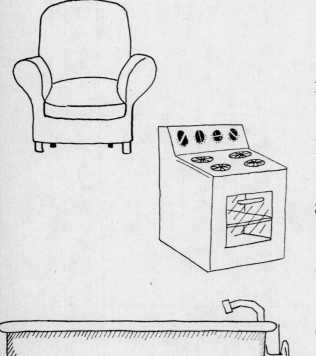

1. sofa

2. stove

3. bathtub

4. refrigerator

5. chair

6. table

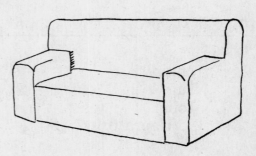

184

Match

apartment   mo.

bedroom   apt.

bathroom   br.

month   ba.

$450 a mo.
1 Br.
1 Ba. apt.

1. How much? _____
2. How many bathrooms? _____
3. How many bedrooms? _____

$395 a mo.
3 Br.
2 Ba.

4. How much? _____
5. How many bedrooms? _____
6. How many bathrooms? _____

For Rent $475
a mo.
Children OK.
4 Br.
2 Ba.

7. How much? _____
8. How many bedrooms? _____
9. How many bathrooms? _____

Date _____

A. Is this house for rent?

B. Yes, it is. It's $260 a month.

A. How many bedrooms?

B. 3.

A. Do you pay utilities?

B. I pay water.
You pay gas and electricity.

A. Can I see it?

B. Yes, you can.

Match

1. lamp

2. bed

3. TV

4. rug

5. toilet

6. table

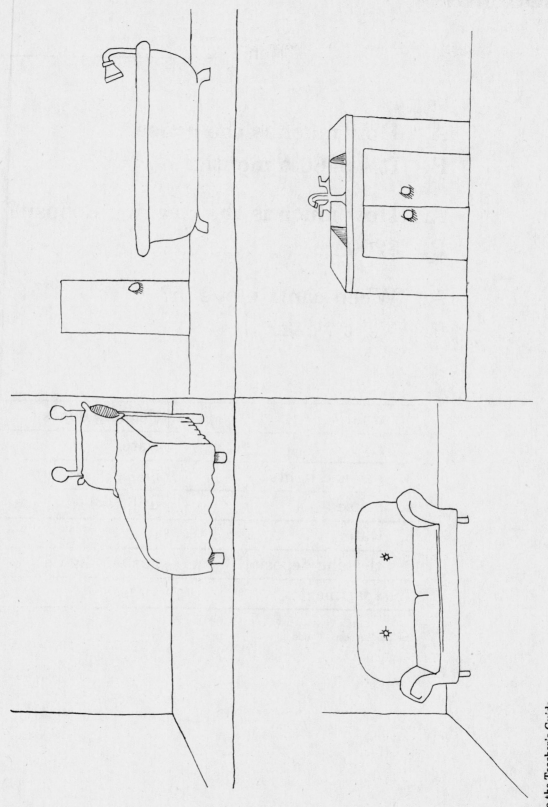

187

HOUSING 6

Name _____

A. How much is the house?
B. It's $460 a month.

A. How much is the cleaning deposit?
B. $200.

A. When can I move in?
B. Next week.

1.	utilities	cleaning deposit
2.	rent	water
3.	gas and lights	house
4.	house	utilities
5.	water	rent
6.	cleaning deposit	gas and lights
7.	apartment	water

See the Teacher's Guide.

HOUSING 7

First name _____

A. My window is broken.
B. Oh, that's too bad.
Call the manager.
A. Why?
B. Because he can fix it.

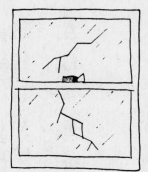

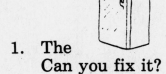
1. The _____ is broken.
Can you fix it?

2. The _____ is broken.
Can you fix it?

3. The _____ is broken.
Can you fix it?

4. The _____ is broken.
Can you fix it?

HOUSING 8

Last name _____

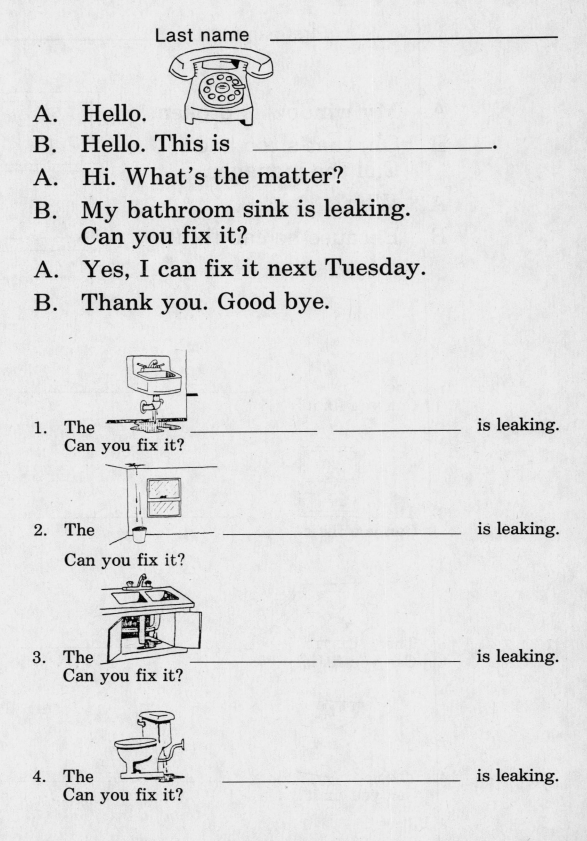

A. Hello.

B. Hello. This is _____.

A. Hi. What's the matter?

B. My bathroom sink is leaking.
    Can you fix it?

A. Yes, I can fix it next Tuesday.

B. Thank you. Good bye.

1. The _____ _____ is leaking.
    Can you fix it?

2. The _____ is leaking.
    Can you fix it?

3. The _____ _____ is leaking.
    Can you fix it?

4. The _____ is leaking.
    Can you fix it?

Address _____

A. Hi. Can I borrow your plunger?

B. Sure. What's wrong?

A. My toilet is stopped up.
   I need to fix it.

| **Can I borrow your** _____? |

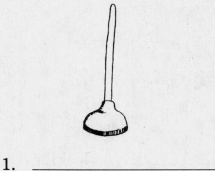

1. _____

2. _____

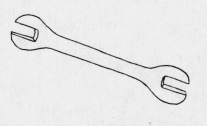

4. _____

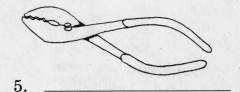

3. _____

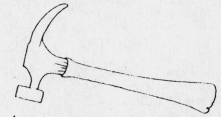

5. _____

1. plunger   4. hammer
2. screwdriver   5. pliers
3. wrench

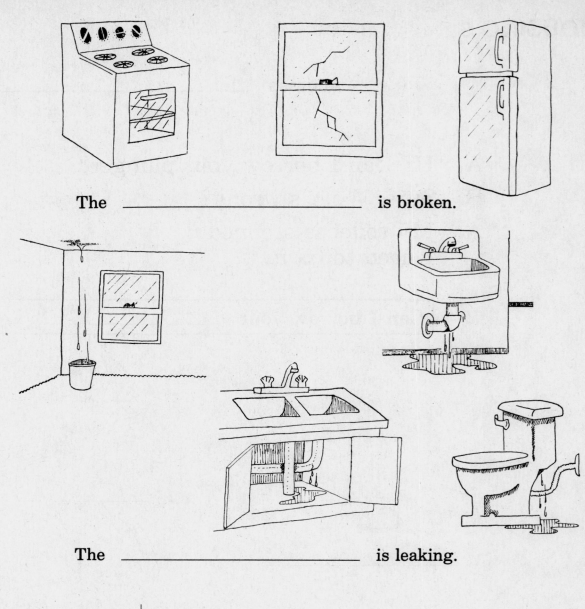

The _____ is broken.

The _____ is leaking.

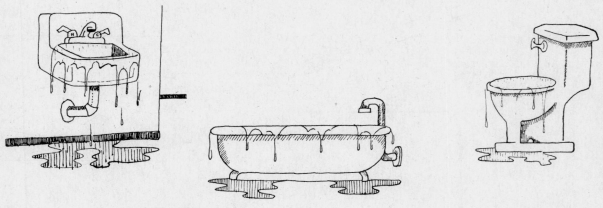

The _____ is stopped up.

stopped up

1. Can I borrow your _____ ?

   My _____ is _____ _____ .

2. Can I borrow your _____ ?

   My _____ is _____ _____ .

broken

3. Can I borrow your _____ ?

   My _____ is _____ .

4. Can I borrow your _____ ?

   My _____ is _____ .

leaking

5. Can I borrow your _____ ?

   My _____ is _____ .

6. Can I borrow your _____ ?

   My _____ is _____ .

Zip code _____

A. Hello.

B. Hello. This is _____.
I have a problem.

A. What's the matter?

B. I have cockroaches in my apartment. Can you spray?

A. Yes, I can.
I can spray next Tuesday.

B. Thanks.

A. You need to go away for 4 hours.

B. OK. Good bye.

A. Bye.

		tomorrow
		next Wednesday
	I can spray	next month
		next week
		this Saturday
		this week

Ann has a problem. She has cockroaches in her kitchen. She has cockroaches in her bathroom, too. She needs to spray.

1. Who has a problem?

   _____.

2. What's the problem?

   _____.

3. Does Ann have cockroaches?

   _____.

4. Where are the cockroaches?

   _____.

5. Does she need to spray?

   _____.

6. Does she have cockroaches in the living room or the kitchen?

   _____.

Do you have _____ **in your**

a

a

a

a

a

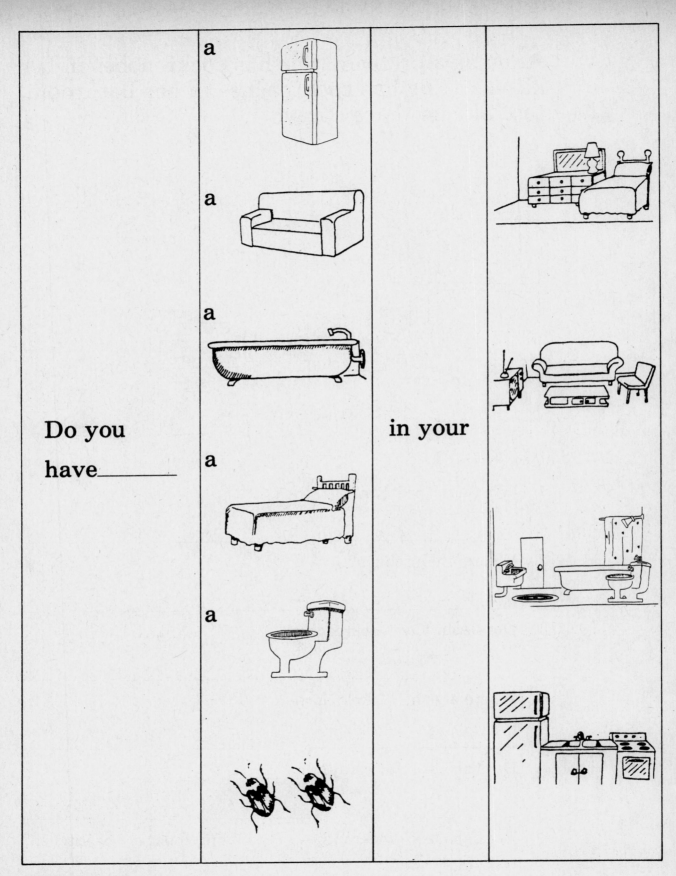

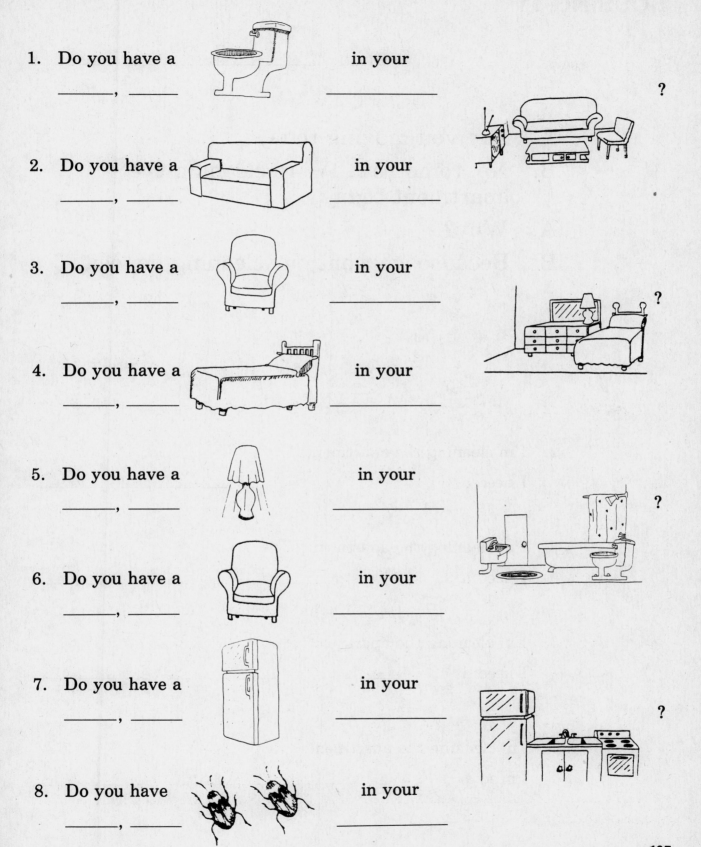

1. Do you have a _____ in your _____, _____ _____ ?

2. Do you have a _____ in your _____, _____ _____

3. Do you have a _____ in your _____, _____ _____

4. Do you have a _____ in your _____, _____ _____

5. Do you have a _____ in your _____, _____ _____

6. Do you have a _____ in your _____, _____ _____

7. Do you have a _____ in your _____, _____ _____ ?

8. Do you have _____ in your _____, _____ _____

State _____

A. Are you moving today?

B. No, tomorrow. We're cleaning the apartment today.

A. Why?

B. Because we want our cleaning deposit.

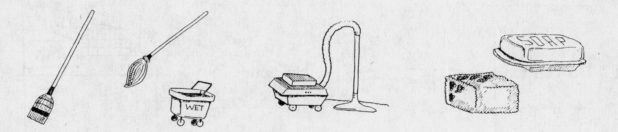

1. I'm cleaning the apartment.

   I need a _____.

2. I'm cleaning the apartment.

   I need a  _____ _____.

3. I'm cleaning the apartment.

   I need a _____ _____ _____.

4. I'm cleaning the apartment.

   I need a _____ _____ _____.

1. What's _____ doing?

_____ _____ _____ _____ .

2. What's _____ doing?

_____ _____ .

3. What's _____ doing?

_____ _____ .

4. What's _____ doing?

_____ _____ _____ _____ .

5. What's _____ doing?

_____ _____ .

Sue and Kim have a new house. It's unfurnished. It has 2 bedrooms and 1 bathroom. Sue and Kim have a sofa, a bed, and a table. They want to buy a refrigerator.

1. Do Sue and Kim have a new house?

   _____.

2. Is it furnished or unfurnished?

   _____.

3. Does it have 2 or 3 bedrooms?

   _____.

4. Do Sue and Kim have a sofa?

   _____.

5. Do Sue and Kim have a bed?

   _____.

6. Do Sue and Kim have a refrigerator?

   _____.

7. Do Sue and Kim want to buy a bed?

   _____.

8. Do Sue and Kim want to buy a table?

   _____.

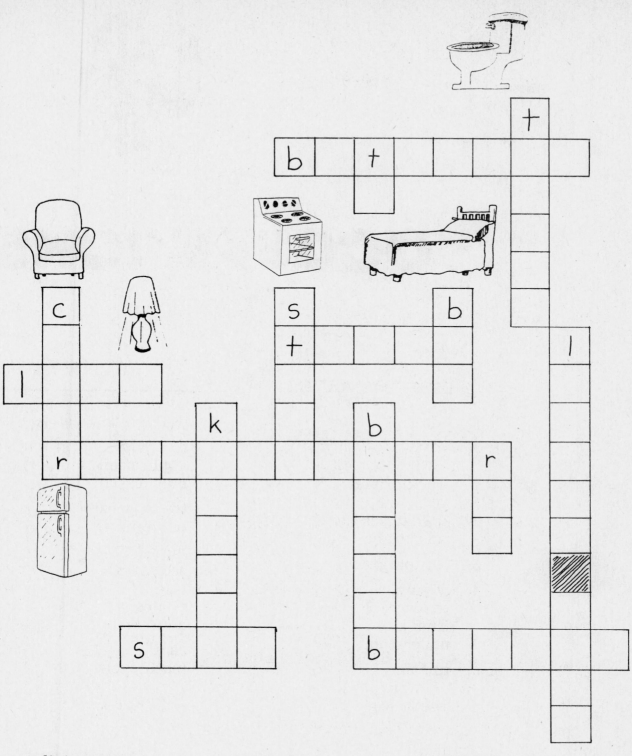

living room
bathroom
bedroom
toilet
stove

bed
rug
lamp
table
t.v.

bathtub
sink
chair
refrigerator
kitchen

OCCUPATIONS

ESSENTIAL VOCABULARY _____

1. job
   cook
   student

2. truck driver
   mechanic
   seamstress
   want to be

3. occupation

4. working
   to learn
   English
   understand

5. full-time
   part-time
   good luck

6. it's nice to meet you

7. to apply
   application
   maybe

8. that's great
   restaurant
   dishes

9. secretary
   salary
   makes
   an hour

10. cars
    motorcycles

homemaker   mechanic   carpenter   cook
student   farmer   plumber   assembler
truck driver   soldier   seamstress   welder
secretary   fisherman   clerk   repairman

OCCUPATIONS 1

 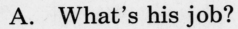 _____

A. What's his job?
B. He's a cook.

A. What's your job?
B. I'm a student.

1. What's her job?

_____ _____ _____.

2. What's his job?

_____ _____ _____.

3. What's her job?

_____ _____ _____.

OCCUPATIONS 2

Telephone _____

A. Is he a truck driver?

B. No, he isn't. He's a mechanic.

A. Is she a cook?

B. No, she isn't. She's a seamstress.

A. Are you a student?

B. Yes, I am. I want to be a _____.

1. Is he a _____?
   Yes, _____ _____.

2. Is he a _____?
   Yes, _____ _____.

3. Is she an _____?
   Yes, _____ _____.

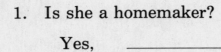

1. Is she a homemaker?

   Yes, _____ _____.

2. Is he a mechanic?

   Yes, _____ _____.

3. Is he a farmer?

   Yes, _____ _____.

4. Is he an assembler?

   No, _____ _____.

5. Is she a farmer?

   No, _____ _____.

6. Is she a soldier?

   No, _____ _____.

OCCUPATIONS 3

Soc. Sec. No. _____

A. Where are you from?

B. I'm from _____.

A. What was your occupation?

B. What?

A. What was your job?

B. I was a _____.

1. What was his occupation?

_____ _____ _____ _____.

2. What was her occupation?

_____ _____ _____ _____.

3. What was his occupation?

_____ _____ _____ _____.

OCCUPATIONS 4

Birth date _____

A. Are you working?

B. No, I'm not.

A. Why?

B. Because I want to learn English.

A. Oh, I understand.

1. Is he working?

   No, _____ _____.

   Why?

   He wants to _____ _____.

2. Is he working?

   Yes, _____ _____.

   What's his job?

   _____ _____ _____.

3. Is she working?

   Yes, _____ _____.

   What's her job?

   _____ _____ _____.

Kim is a student now. He was a soldier in Vietnam. Kim goes to school every day. He studies English. He wants to be a welder.

1. Who's a student?

   _____.

2. Who was a soldier?

   _____.

3. Where is Kim from?

   _____.

4. What was his job?

   _____.

5. What's his job now?

   _____.

6. Is he a welder?

   _____.

7. Is he a fisherman?

   _____.

8. Is he a mechanic?

   _____.

9. Is he a cook?

   _____.

10. Is he a student?

   _____.

OCCUPATIONS 5

Age _____

A.   Are you working?
B.   No, I'm not. I'm looking for a job.

A.   Full-time or part-time?
B.   Part-time.

A.   Good luck.
B.   Thanks.

He isn't working.
He's looking for a job.
He wants to work full-time.

1.   Is he working? _____ _____ _____.

2.   Is he looking for a job?

_____ _____ _____.

3.   Does he want full-time or part-time?

_____.

Who	Was	Is

OCCUPATIONS 6

Signature _____

A. This is my friend, _____ .
    He's looking for a job.
B. It's nice to meet you _____ .
C. It's nice to meet you, too.

Ann

A. This is my friend, _____ .
B. It's _____ _____ _____ _____ ,
    _____ .

Bob

A. This is my friend, _____ .
B. It's _____ _____ _____ _____ ,
    _____ .

Kim

A. This is my friend, _____ .
B. It's _____ _____ _____ _____ ,
    _____ .

Lee

A. This is my friend, _____ .
B. It's _____ _____ _____ _____ ,
    _____ .

Bob Jones wants to apply for a job. He has the application. His address is 3617 Main Street, San Diego, California. His zip code is 92110. He's 35 years old. His birth date is May 17, 1948.

JOB APPLICATION

Last name _____ First name _____

Address _____ City _____

State _____ Zip code _____

Age _____ Birth date _____

Bob Jones is from Mexico. His social security number is 560-58-8025. He's married. He has 4 children. He was a mechanic in Mexico.

Social Security Number   -   -

Sex   male ☐   female ☐   Married   yes ☐   no ☐

Children   yes ☐   no ☐   How many _____

Where are you from?

What was your job?

Signature _____

Date _____

OCCUPATIONS 7

Date _____

A. I want to apply for a job.
B. Here's the application.
   Please fill it out.
A. Can I return it tomorrow?
B. Yes, you can.

A. Can I help you?
B. Yes, I want to return my job application.
A. Thank you.
B. Can I come for an interview?
A. Maybe; we'll call you.
B. OK. Thank you.

JOB APPLICATION

Last name _____ First name _____

Address _____ City _____

State _____ Zip code _____

Age _____ Date of birth _____

Social Security Number _____ - ___ - _____

Sex male ☐ Married yes ☐
    female ☐   no ☐

Children yes ☐ How many _____
         no ☐

Birthplace

What was your job?

Signature _____

     Date _____

Name _____

A. I have a new job.

B. That's great!
   What do you do?

A. I work in a restaurant.

B. Do you wash dishes?

A. No, I don't. I cook.

A. She has a new job.

B. What does she do?

A. She sews.

A. He has a new job.

B. What does he do?

A. He fixes cars.

1. He's a _____.
   _____ fishes.

2. She's a _____.
   _____ sews.

3. _____ a _____ _____.
   _____ drives a truck.

4. _____ a _____.
   _____ fixes leaking sinks.

5. _____ a _____.
   _____ writes letters.

6. _____ a _____.
   _____ builds houses.

OCCUPATIONS 9

First name _____

A. Is she a secretary?
B. Yes, she is.
A. What's her salary?
B. It's $800.00 a month.
A. Is he a cook?
B. Yes, he is. He makes $5.60 an hour.

1.
Cook wanted
$7.00 an hour
Part-time
292–1111

2.
Seamstress
needed
$5.00 an hour
731–2864

3.
Mechanic
wanted
Full-time
$190.00 a week

	Job	Salary	Part-time / Full-time	Phone number
1.				
2.				
3.				

OCCUPATIONS 10

Last name _____

A. My son wants a job.
B. What can he do?
A. He can fix cars.
B. Can he fix motorcycles, too?
A. Yes, he can. He's a mechanic.

1. She's a _____.
    _____ can write letters.

2. She's a _____.
    _____ can cook.

3. He's a _____.
    _____ can farm.

Juan was a mechanic in Mexico. He's a student now. He's looking for a job. He can fix cars. He can work part-time.

1. Who was a mechanic?

   _____.

2. Who's a student now?

   _____.

3. Was Juan a mechanic in Mexico?

   _____.

4. Is Juan a student now?

   _____.

5. Is Juan looking for a job?

   _____.

6. What can he do?

   _____.

7. Can he fix cars?

   _____.

8. Can he work part-time?

   _____.

9. Can he work full-time?

   _____.

10. What was his job?

   _____.

mechanic
cook
welder
homemaker
student
soldier
clerk
farmer
assembler
fisherman
seamstress

10
COMMUNITY

ESSENTIAL VOCABULARY _____

1. bank
   hurry up

2. to cash
   check
   identification
   ID
   credit card
   green card

3. endorse
   on the back

4. dollar
   quarters

5. dimes
   nickel
   pay phone
   out of order

6. I'll call later
   wrong number

7. post office
   to mail
   letter
   stamps
   money order
   aerogramme

8. in line

9. emergency services
   on fire
   nearest cross street
   I don't know
   fire truck

10. drank
    poison
    ambulance
    choking
    bleeding
    accident

11. stolen
police

12. police officer
someone
beat up
speak

13. bill
advertisement
throw it away

14. gas and electric
service charge
total

15. library card
sign

1.

2.

3.

4.

5.

6.

fire fighter, fire truck
mail carrier, post office
library

police officer
bank
courtesy booth

COMMUNITY 1

Address _____

A. Hello.

B. Hi.

A. Where are you going?

B. I'm going to the bank.

A. Is it open?

B. Yes, it opens at 10:00 and closes at 5:00.

A. Oh, hurry up. It's 4:30 now.

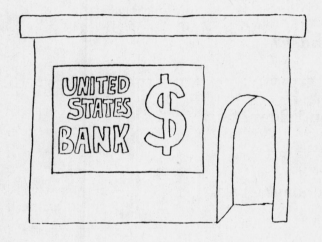

	open	closed
Mon.	10:00	5:00
Tue.	10:00	5:00
Wed.	10:00	5:00
Thur.	10:00	5:00
Fri.	10:00	8:00
Sat.	9:00	12:00
Sun.	CLOSED	

1. What time does the bank open on Tuesday?

   _____.

2. What time does the bank open on Saturday?

   _____.

3. What time does the bank close on Friday?

   _____.

Store Hours	
Sun.	closed
Mon.	10–5
Tues.	10–5
Wed.	10–5
Thurs.	9–5
Fri.	9–7
Sat.	9–1

1. Is the store open on Monday?

   _____, _____ _____.

2. What time is it open on Monday?

   _____.

3. Is the store open on Friday?

   _____, _____ _____.

4. What time is it open on Friday?

   _____.

5. Is the store open on Sunday?

   _____, _____ _____.

6. When is it open on Saturday?

   _____–_____.

7. When is it open on Tuesday?

   _____–_____.

8. When is it open on Wednesday?

   _____–_____.

Zip code _____

A. Next.
B. I want to cash my check.
A. Do you have identification?
B. What?
A. Do you have ID?
B. Oh. Yes, I do.

ID card   Driver's license

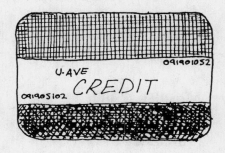

1. _____   2. _____

Credit card

3. _____

State _____

A. I want to cash this check.
    Here's my ID.

B. It's $3.00 to cash a check.

A. $3.00?

B. Yes, $3.00.

A. Oh, OK.

B. Please endorse the check.

A. What?

B. Write your name on the back.

_____
| _____ 19_____ |
| Pay to the   _____ |
| order of _____ $ | | |
| _____|_____| |
| |
| _____ Dollars |
| |
| _____ |
|_____|

date: May 31, 1984   how much: 10.00

to: Ann Lee   ten

from: Bob Jones

```
                                   June 18   19 84
Pay to the
order of    Gas and Electric        $ 54.98
Fifty-four and 98/100 ――――――――――――     Dollars


            Ann Lee
```

1. Who's it to? _____
2. Who's it from? _____
3. How much? _____
4. What's the date? _____

```
                                   Dec. 3   19 83
Pay to the
order of    Telephone Company      $ 13.67
Thirteen and 67/100 ――――――――――――     Dollars



            Bob Jones
```

5. Who's it to? _____
6. Who's it from? _____
7. How much? _____
8. What's the date? _____

_____ 19____

Pay to the
order of _____ $[   ]

_____ Dollars

_____

_____ 19____

Pay to the
order of _____ $[   ]

_____ Dollars

_____

_____ 19____

Pay to the
order of _____ $[   ]

_____ Dollars

_____

Mr. Jones is in the bank. He has a check. He wants to cash the check. He wants money. He's endorsing the check on the back.

1. Where's Mr. Jones?

   _____.

2. Does he have a check?

   _____.

3. Does he want to cash a check?

   _____.

4. Does he want money?

   _____.

5. Where does he endorse the check?

   _____.

6. Who's in the bank?

   _____.

7. What does he have?

   _____.

8. Please sign your name.

   _____.

9. Please write your name.

   _____.

COMMUNITY 4

City _____

A. Excuse me. Do you have change for a dollar?

B. What do you need?

A. I need 4 quarters.

B. Let me see. Sorry, I don't.

A. Thanks, anyway.

1¢   5¢   10¢   25¢

---

1.   = _____30¢_____

---

2.   = _____ ¢

---

3.   = _____ ¢

COMMUNITY 5

Telephone _____

A.   Do you have change for a quarter?
B.   Yes, I do. I have 2 dimes and a nickel.
A.   Thanks. Do you have a pay phone?
B.   Yes, but it's out of order.

1.   = ___26___ ¢

2.   = _____ ¢

3.   = _____ ¢

4.   = _____ ¢

5.   = _____ ¢

Soc. Sec. No. _____

A. Hello.

B. Hello, this is _____.
Is Bob home?

A. No, he isn't. He's at school.

B. Thank you. I'll call later. Good bye.

A. Good bye.

A. Hello.

B. Hello, this is _____.
Is Ann home?

A. Sorry. You have the wrong number.

B. Is this 423–5179?

A. No, it isn't.

B. Sorry, good bye.

A. Bye.

COMMUNITY 7

A. I'm going to the post office.
   I need to mail a letter.

B. Can I come? I need to buy stamps.

A. OK. Let's go.

  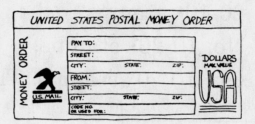 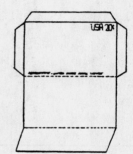

1. I'm going to the _____ _____.

2. I need to mail a  _____.

3. I'm going to the _____ _____.

4. I need to buy _____.

5. I'm going to the _____ _____.

6. I need to buy a _____ _____.

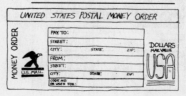

7. I'm going to the _____ _____.

8. I need to buy an 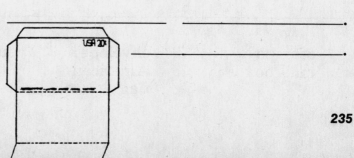 _____.

COMMUNITY 8

Age _____

A. Are you in line?

B. Yes.

A. You're next.

B. I want to buy 10 20¢ stamps.

A. 20 10¢ stamps?

B. No, 10 20¢ stamps.

A. Oh, 10 20¢ stamps. That's $2.00.

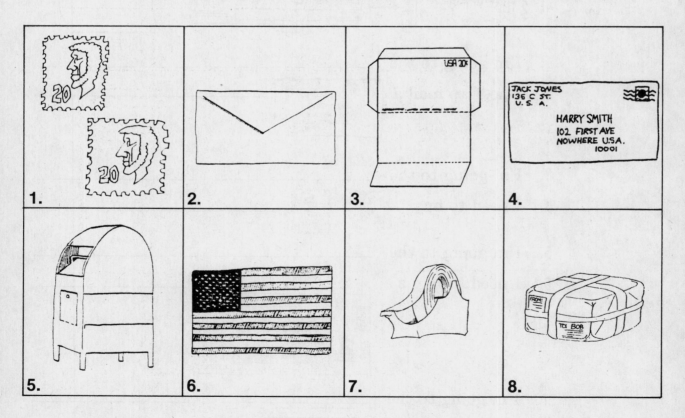

stamps	envelope	aerogramme	letter
mail box	American flag	tape	package

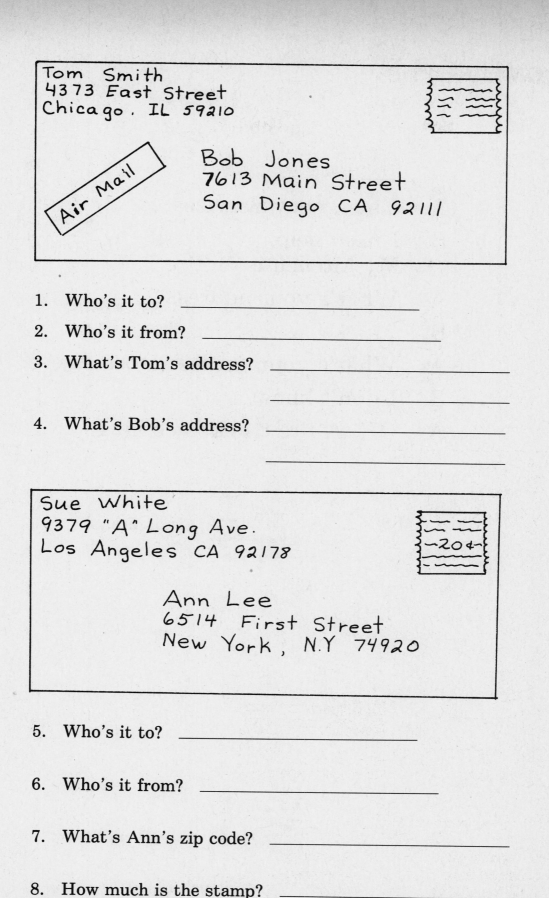

Tom Smith
4373 East Street
Chicago, IL 59210

Air Mail

Bob Jones
7613 Main Street
San Diego CA 92111

1. Who's it to? _____

2. Who's it from? _____

3. What's Tom's address? _____

_____

4. What's Bob's address? _____

_____

Sue White
9379 "A" Long Ave.
Los Angeles CA 92178

20¢

Ann Lee
6514 First Street
New York, N.Y 74920

5. Who's it to? _____

6. Who's it from? _____

7. What's Ann's zip code? _____

8. How much is the stamp? _____

COMMUNITY 9

Signature _____

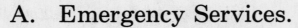

911

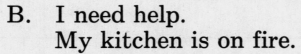

A. Emergency Services.

B. I need help.
   My kitchen is on fire.

A. What's your address?

B. _____.

A. What's your nearest cross street?

B. I don't know.

A. OK. A fire truck is coming.

1. My 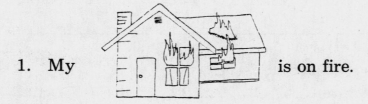 is on fire.

2. My  is on fire.

3. My is on fire.

238

COMMUNITY 10

Date _____

911

A. Emergency Services.

B. This is an emergency.
My son drank poison.

A. What's your name?

B. _____.

A. What's your address?

B. _____.

A. What's your nearest cross street?

B. _____.

A. OK. An ambulance is coming.

B. Thank you.

1. choking   **2.** accident   **3.** poison   **4.** bleeding

COMMUNITY 11

A. My purse was stolen.

B. Oh no! Call the police.

A. What's the number?

B. _____

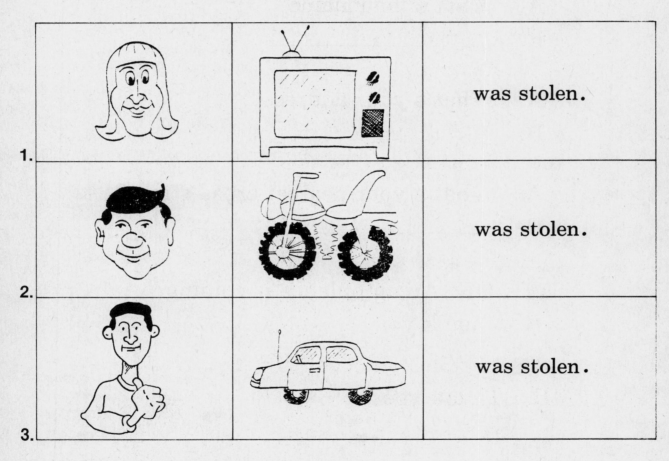

1.   ...   was stolen.

2.   ...   was stolen.

3.   ...   was stolen.

4. My name is _____.

5. My address is _____.

6. My telephone number is _____.

7. My cross street is _____.

COMMUNITY 12

Address _____

911

A. Emergency Services.
B. Hello. I need a police officer.
   This is an emergency.

A. What's the matter?
B. Someone beat up my son.
   I'm from _____.
   I speak _____.

A. What's your name?
B. _____

A. What's your address?
B. _____

A. A police officer is coming.
B. Thank you.

COMMUNITY 13

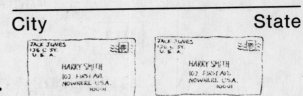

A. Here's the mail.

B. This is a bill. I need to pay it.

A. Is this a bill?

B. No, it isn't. It's an advertisement.
    Throw it away.

Bayside Telephone Company   From 3–28 To 4–28

Bob Jones   Account   Number   8377–664–921
3613 Main St.
San Diego, CA

         Monthly Service Charge $10.88
                 U.S. Tax   .64
                 Total $11.52

Payment for current charges is due June 13.

---

1. Who's it to? _____

2. Who's it from? _____

3. How much is the bill? _____

4. When is it due? _____

State   Zip code

A. Can I pay my gas and electric bill here?

B. Yes, you can.

A. How much is the service charge?

B. 50¢. Let me see your bill.
   It's $44.00. The total is $44.50.

191567823001	7613 Main St.	Total $39.28

Pirate Gas and Electric Co.
Service from 7–28 to 8–28

Gas	26 Therms	12.56
Elec.	258 KWHR	26.05
Gas Franchise Fee		.13
Elec. Franchise Fee		.54
Due Sept. 22, 1984		Total $39.28

1. How much is the bill? _____

2. When is it due? _____

3. Who is it from? _____

_____
Birth date   Age

A. Can I help you?

B. Yes, I want this book.

A. Do you have a library card?

B. No, I don't.

A. Do you have ID?

B. Yes, I do.

A. OK. I can give you a card. Here it is. Sign your name.

LIBRARY CARD	
Name _____	
Address _____	
_____	
Signature _____	
Telephone	Driver's lic. no.
Parent's signature	

1. Do you have a library card?

    _____

2. Do you go to the library?

    _____

Kim likes the library. He likes to read. He has a library card. He can take books home. Some books are difficult. Some books are easy. He can read the easy books now.

1. Does Kim like the library?

   _____.

2. Does Kim like to read?

   _____.

3. Does Kim have a library card?

   _____.

4. Can Kim take books home?

   _____.

5. Can Kim read easy books?

   _____.

6. Can you read easy books?

   _____.

7. Do you like to read?

   _____.

8. Do you like the library?

   _____.

9. Do you have a library card?

   _____.

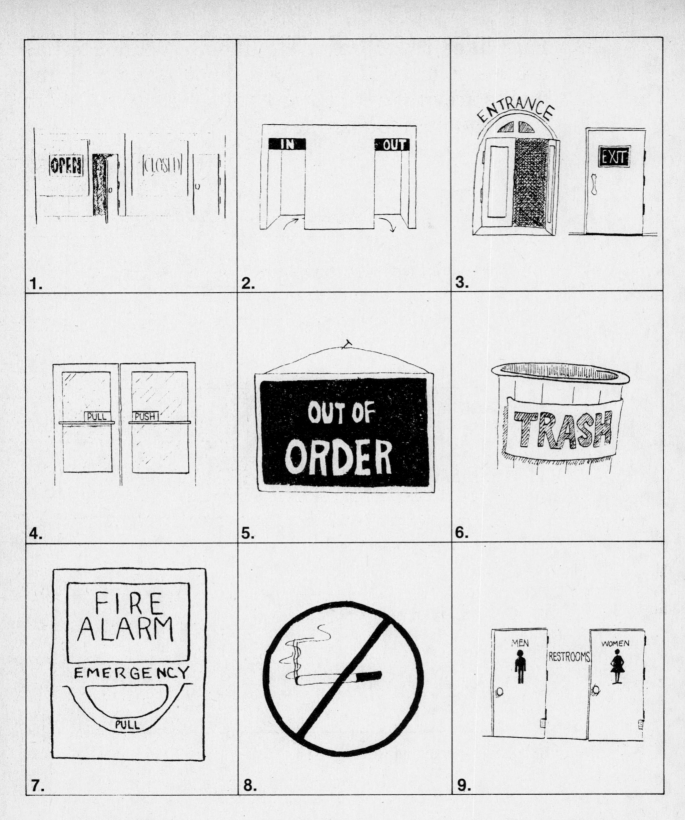

open/closed
push/pull
fire alarm

in/out
out of order
no smoking

entrance/exit
trash
men/women